D1411553

LIVING
IN AN
IMPERFECT WORLD

LIVING
IN AN
IMPERFECT WORLD

by
Dr. R. B. Ouellette

Post Office Box 1099 • Murfreesboro, Tennessee 37133

To my lovely and wonderful wife, Krisy:
Thanks for 31 years of love, devotion and support.
Special thanks for your enthusiastic encouragement
in this project. I love you.

Printed and Bound in the United States of America

Contents

Acknowledgments

This book would still be a collection of cassette tapes gathering dust if it had not been for the exceptional work of Bob Byers. He is a tremendously talented editor and transcriber. My gratitude should also be expressed to the wonderful people of First Baptist Church of Bridgeport, whom it has been my privilege to serve and lead for 29 years and for whose benefit these lessons were originally written.

Chapter 1
Dealing With Injustice

Jim MacLaren didn't get an even break. At the age of twenty-two, the Yale graduate seemed to have everything going for him. He excelled in his studies, as a football player and as an actor. But one balmy night his motorcycle was hit by a twenty-ton bus.

He was thought to be dead on arrival at the hospital. But the heroic efforts of the emergency room staff saved his life, and he recovered—mostly. Jim lost his left leg below the knee.

He didn't let that stop him. He spent the next eight years becoming one of the best one-legged athletes in the world. Within the first year his brutal rehab regimen had him ready to complete 10K races. He set new records for disabled athletes in the New York and Boston marathons.

That wasn't enough for Jim. He began competing in triathlons. The triathlete swims 2.4 miles, then bikes 112 miles and finishes by running a full 26.2-mile marathon. Jim did that on one leg.

Then when things seemed to be going so well, disaster struck again. While Jim was competing in a triathlon in Los Angeles in 1993, a van was mistakenly allowed onto the street where the bicyclists were riding. The van hit Jim head on,

1

flinging him across the street into a lamp post. The impact snapped his neck and left Jim paralyzed.

Confined to a wheelchair, Jim lived with constant pain. The nerves to his arms and legs were not completely severed, leaving him subject to spastic fits. After being in a steel halo for three months, he began a new course of rehabilitation at a special center in Colorado.

After just six months he was living independently and giving motivational speeches. But depression set in when he came to the realization that he would never be free from pain and, no matter how hard he worked, he would never walk again.

Jim won a $3.8 million settlement for the accident and moved to Kona, Hawaii. Soon he was addicted to cocaine and wallowing in self-pity. One night as he rolled in his wheelchair down a street where he had once raced in marathons, he looked up to the sky and yelled, "Why are You doing this to me?" Jim MacLaren was fed up with injustice. How would he respond?

∞∞∞

The people who make up my church are some of the greatest people in the world. I love them, and I'm thankful for the privilege of being their pastor. I wish I could make it so they never were sad. I wish I could make it so they never had any burdens to bear. I wish I could wipe away all the hard times and all the unfair and unjust things they have to face in life. But I can't do that.

I can't do it for my church members, and I can't do it for you. Job said, "Man is born unto trouble, as the sparks fly upward" (Job 5:7). Jesus said, "In the world ye shall have tribulation" (John 16:33). He said, "The servant is not greater than his lord. If they have persecuted me, they will also persecute you" (John 15:20).

"It is impossible," our Lord declared, "but that offences will come" (Luke 17:1). Jesus made it very clear that since we are living in an imperfect world, we should expect to face difficulties and troubles.

One of the best examples of dealing with injustice in the Bible is the story of Joseph.

"Now Israel loved Joseph more than all his children, because he was the son of his old age: and he made him a coat of many colours.

"And when his brethren saw that their father loved him more than all his brethren, they hated him, and could not speak peaceably unto him. "—Gen. 37:3,4.

The coat that Jacob gave Joseph was worn by people who were in positions of authority. It was the sign of a person who did not do the menial labor of others, but gave orders. Jacob showed favoritism to Joseph. He was unjust in his treatment of his other sons.

Have you ever been treated unjustly? Can you say that everything that has happened to you was exactly right? Can you say that nobody ever did wrong to you? None of us can say that.

I. The Reality of Injustice

All of us suffer from injustice in one form or another. This is what I call the reality of injustice.

In History

There is injustice throughout history. As I read Scripture, I find injustice. Joseph was treated unjustly by his brothers. Daniel was treated unjustly by those who opposed him for no other reason than he did right and told the truth and loved God. He was thrown into a den of lions when he had done nothing for which to be blamed except to pray.

David was treated unjustly by Saul, who pursued him and

tried to take his life. Yet David had done nothing to deserve the death penalty. Herod was unjust when he killed all the male babies two years of age and under so that he could destroy the One who was born King of the Jews.

Scriptural history is filled with injustice. Secular history is filled with injustice as well. I don't know anybody who wouldn't admit that slavery was unjust. It's wrong for a man to own another man. Yet slavery was practiced for centuries. In fact, they tell us that there are still places in the world where slavery continues.

During World War II, people whose only "crime" was that they were of Japanese descent were put in internment camps. Some had been born in the United States of America and didn't even speak Japanese. But when the war with Japan started, fear made us lock up those people. That was unjust.

I've studied enough to know that the American Indians were not all noble, and the white men were not all evil. But it is also true that the Indians were not all evil and the white men were not all noble. The historical record is that many of the treaties that our government made with the Indian people were broken and violated. Secular history is full of injustice. People have not treated others fairly.

From the Heathen

The heathen people who fill our world are often unjust. I preached some time ago in Central Lake, Michigan. A preacher was there from Akron, Ohio. He told me how his church had a building they had bought when they were getting started.

When they had outgrown that building and needed to move, they sold the building to a lawyer. The lawyer agreed that he would pay them $250,000. They signed the contract and received a down payment of $25,000. Then the lawyer turned around and sued them, saying they'd somehow misrepresented things and hadn't done things right.

4

Knowing the ins and outs of the legal system, he used his knowledge against them. The only money they ever collected from the quarter-million-dollar sale of their church building was the down payment of $25,000. It was unjust.

In Our Homes

Injustice in history and from the heathen is bad enough. But frequently in our own homes, among our own families, we find that there is injustice. Maybe your parents loved your brother or sister more than they loved you. Perhaps they treated you unjustly.

In the case of Jacob and his sons, the injustice was very real. Jacob loved Joseph more than all his brethren. Notice the wording of the Scripture at the beginning of this chapter. It doesn't say, "Israel loved Joseph more than *any of* his children." It says, "Israel loved Joseph more than *all* his children."

Jacob loved Joseph more than all his other sons put together. There was real injustice in the family. Jacob not only felt favoritism toward Joseph, he showed it. Every time Joseph's brothers saw him in the coat of many colors, it was a reminder that their father was unfair and unjust.

II. The Roots of Injustice

Now let's look at the roots of injustice. There are always reasons that people behave unjustly. People act the way they do because of something that has happened to them.

Unfairness

The first root cause is that life is unfair.

Let me tell you about my mother-in-law and Christmas presents. She spends $20 on each member of the family for Christmas gifts. If you get a gift from her, you know it cost $20. If your gift was $20 and another received a gift that was $17.50, he will get a $2.50 pair of socks or a $2.50 jar of peanuts.

There's a name for those gifts in my wife's family—"evener-uppers." I doubt that phrase will ever make it into the dictionary, but that's what we call it. Mom's going to be sure that she is exactly fair and just with each member of her family. We all know that. Sometimes you'll hear one of us say, "Mom gave me an 'evener-upper' gift." But most people are not like my mother-in-law.

Jacob didn't do things that way. He was unfair in the way he treated his sons. He was blatant in his favoritism. He placed his younger son Joseph in charge of his ten older brothers and gave him extra love. Because his other sons saw Jacob's unfairness, they too became unjust. They put Joseph in a pit and then sold him to a caravan of Midianite slave traders. Jacob's sons felt—aptly so—as if they had been treated unfairly. And because their father had been unfair to them, they rationalized that it was all right for them to be unjust to Joseph.

We see in this story the vicious cycle that injustice can cause. Children learn what they live. When their parents are unjust, children feel they too have the right to be unjust. They "do unto others" as it has been done to them.

Our society is ready with quick excuses for those who do wrong. Someone will say, "Well, he was brought up in a dysfunctional family," or, "He abuses children because he was abused as a child," or, "She can't help it. The circumstances of her life are to blame."

There's an element of truth in that—such things can influence us. If we are not careful, the injustices that have been brought upon us will work themselves out in our lives, and we will treat other people as unjustly as we have been treated. However, we must remember that the sins of others do not excuse us in the eyes of God.

Unawareness

Unfairness can be a root cause of injustice, but a more

significant root cause is: our unawareness that God is in control of everything.

I'm not saying God causes what happens to us. And I'm certainly not saying He is responsible for it. What I am saying is, He uses even unjust and unfair things for our good.

God uses the wrath of man to praise Him (Ps. 76:10). He can take the most terrible injustices in our lives and use them for His glory.

Each of us needs to understand that no one can keep us from doing the will of God. No one can keep you from enjoying the blessing of God or keep you from accomplishing what God wants you to accomplish—except you. Your response to injustice, not the injustice itself, determines the effect it will have on your life.

Joseph understood this principle. After being sold as a slave and unjustly imprisoned, he would look back years later and say to his brothers, 'You may have meant it for evil, but God meant it for good.'

If we are unaware that God is at work in our lives, we can easily fall victim to bitterness because of the actions of others. But an equally great danger is that by allowing ourselves to become bitter, we will defile the lives of others by perpetuating the cycle of injustice.

Hebrews 12:15–17 talks about the effect bitterness can have on our lives:

"Looking diligently lest any man fail of the grace of God; lest any root of bitterness springing up trouble you, and thereby many be defiled;

"Lest there be any fornicator, or profane person, as Esau, who for one morsel of meat sold his birthright.

"For ye know how that afterward, when he would have inherited the blessing, he was rejected: for he found no place of repentance, though he sought it carefully with tears."

7

You may think Esau was a bitter person and the cause of his troubles. But Esau is not the example of the bitter person. He is the example of one defiled by a bitter person.

Rebekah received a promise from God when her twin sons were born. Esau was born first; Jacob, second. God said, "The elder shall serve the younger" (Gen. 25:23). As the boys grew, Esau had a great affinity for his father Isaac. Both were outdoorsmen. They shared a love of hunting. Isaac loved Esau.

The Bible says, "Jacob was a plain man, dwelling in tents." I think that's Hebrew for "Momma's boy." Jacob stayed home with Rebekah. She loved him and in her heart nourished the promise God had given that her darling, her favorite, would be promoted.

The problem was, God was not working on her schedule. She wasn't getting what she longed for. She allowed herself to become bitter, and that bitterness defiled Esau.

When Isaac thought he was about to die, he said to Esau, "Give me one last good meal, and I'll give you the blessing." Hearing that, Rebekah's bitterness overflowed. I can imagine her saying, "God promised that Jacob, my favorite, would be in charge. Now all my old, blind and feeble husband is worried about is his belly. He has forgotten about the promise of God and is going to give the blessing to Esau, not to Jacob."

So she decided to take into her own hands what God had promised He would do, to take to herself the authority that belongs to God. What did she do? She made a liar out of her son. She took advantage of his weak and scheming nature. Together Rebekah and Jacob deceived Isaac into giving Jacob the blessing instead of Esau.

What was the end result? Esau rightly felt that his mother had mistreated him. He did not see the hand of God putting Jacob in charge. All he could see was that his mother's manipulation got Jacob the blessing. He blamed Rebekah.

III. Responding to Injustice

How should we respond to injustice?

Personal Response

Sometimes we respond personally. That is, we take the injustice as a personal affront. Instead of seeing that God can use what happened to us, we decide we're going to get even. When an injustice is perpetrated against us or against somebody we love, we decide to get back at them or get even with them. People often excuse this wrong behavior, saying, "That's the way it was when I was growing up, so it's all right for me to be that way." But responding personally guarantees that we will perpetuate the cycle of injustice.

Principled Response

The other option that we have when faced with injustice is to respond according to principle. Instead of responding personally, we can act according to the principles we find in the Word of God. I find four guidelines for our proper response in the story of Joseph.

Recognize your responsibility. Joseph was sold by his brothers to be a slave. They were jealous of him because their father showed favoritism toward him. Jacob was unfair by not giving equal treatment to his children.

Joseph's brothers excused their unjust treatment of Joseph because of Jacob's unfairness. And if things had followed their normal course, Joseph would have been unjust to the people with whom he dealt. Then those people would have been unjust to others in turn. The whole vicious cycle of wrong behavior would have been repeated again and again.

Joseph was faced with a choice: Would he continue the cycle of injustice, or would he break it by doing what was right? Would he respond personally, or would he respond according to principle?

The world thinks we are justified in being unjust if somebody did wrong in their treatment of us. Our leaders excuse the behavior of those who have been mistreated. We are told, "You shouldn't expect anything better of them. It's really not their fault. It's society's fault."

Get suspicious when someone wants to blame a group for the behavior of an individual. That is exactly the opposite of what the Bible says. The Bible says until individuals change, society will never change. God's way of dealing with the problems of society is one heart at a time. God deals with people, not groups. The Bible says, "So then every one of us shall give account of himself to God" (Rom. 14:12). God does not excuse our wrong behavior because of someone else's wrong behavior.

There are two common mistakes in the way most people respond to problems: They want to blame somebody else for their problems, or they want to blame themselves for someone else's behavior.

Neither of those approaches is right. Now don't misunderstand me; there are responsibilities. Whenever two people have a problem, it's likely that both are at fault. There may be varying levels of responsibility, but it is almost always shared.

In counselling a married couple, I often say to the wife: "Nothing your husband has done is responsible for anything you have done. And nothing that you have done is an excuse for anything that your husband has done." And I tell the husband the same thing. We bear full responsibility for how we respond and act.

Although you may be a part of the cycle of injustice because of what others have done to you, by the grace of God you can break it. That's what Joseph did.

"And he [Potiphar] left all that he had in Joseph's hand; and he knew not ought he had, save the bread which he did eat. And Joseph was a goodly person, and well favoured.

"And it came to pass after these things, that his master's wife cast her eyes upon Joseph; and she said, Lie with me.

"But he refused, and said unto his master's wife, Behold, my master wotteth [knows] *not what is with me in the house, and he hath committed all that he hath to my hand;*

"There is none greater in this house than I; neither hath he kept back any thing from me but thee, because thou art his wife."—Gen. 39:6–9.

Joseph was presented with an opportunity to act unjustly. It wasn't fair for Potiphar to own him. Therefore, by the kind of reasoning we often use, he would have been justified to sin with Potiphar's wife. But Joseph understood the principle of responsibility.

Joseph knew to whom Mrs. Potiphar belonged, and he said, "Thou art his wife: how then can I do this great wickedness, and sin against God?" Joseph also knew to whom he belonged. He was saying, "You belong to him, and I belong to God. And what you are proposing cannot happen."

By his nature, man lives a backward Golden Rule: Do unto others as they have done unto you. Sometimes we even get a little proactive in the backward Golden Rule, and we do unto others *before* they do unto us. But Jesus said, "Therefore all things whatsoever ye would that men should do to you, do ye even so to them" (Matt. 7:12).

Don't get trapped into that cycle of injustice generation after generation after generation. Don't ever use that for an excuse. If you believe you can't help it, because that's the way you were raised and that's the way you are, then you might as well close this book right now, stop reading your Bible and give up on going to church. If God can't change us, there's no hope for us.

But there is hope. God can change us. We are not doomed to repeat the wrongs of others. Joseph broke the pattern of injustice, and so can you.

He was confronted with temptation. We would understand on a human level if he had said, "Yeah, why not? God seems to have abandoned me, my brothers have rejected me, my father hasn't been able to deliver me. Nobody here knows about me or about my God. Nobody here speaks my language. Nobody will ever know. Why not?"

But instead of giving in to temptation, Joseph said, "How...can I do this great wickedness, and sin against God?" He recognized his responsibility to be faithful, to do what he knew was right, whether or not right had been done to him. Joseph was faithful to God in Potiphar's house.

Then when Potiphar's wife falsely accused him, he was put into prison. Now he had even more excuse to treat others unfairly. But in the prison, Joseph continued to be faithful. And because of his faithfulness, he was promoted, just as he had been in Potiphar's house.

Pharaoh, upset with his butler and baker, had put them in the same prison with Joseph. Each had a dream. Joseph saw their troubled faces and asked what the problem was. They said, "We have dreamed a dream, and there is no interpreter of it. And Joseph said unto them, Do not interpretations belong to God? tell me them, I pray you" (Gen. 40:8).

Joseph could have said, "I think I can tell you what your dreams mean. I've been able to do this before." If he had been like some people I know, he might even have said, "I'll pray about it and let you know what I come up with."

But what he said was, "Do not interpretations belong to God?" Joseph always pointed back to God because he understood that all things belong to God and that God was always with him. Joseph accepted his responsibility for his reactions. Joseph was faithful to God in the prison.

Our number one responsibility is to be faithful to God, no matter what comes. Here is where we often mess up. We get our focus on people and off God. We think we have something to *prove*. Instead, we have Someone we need to *please*.

Refuse to retaliate. God gave Joseph the meaning of Pharaoh's dream, and Joseph gave it to Pharaoh. Pharaoh then placed Joseph in charge of Egypt's preparations for the coming famine. Joseph was second in command of the most powerful nation on earth.

When the famine came, no one could buy food without Joseph's approval. After a while, the people in other countries affected by the famine heard that there was bread in the land of Egypt.

Approximately twenty years after Joseph was sold into slavery, his brothers came to Egypt to buy food. He recognized them, but they didn't recognize him. That was the last place they expected to see Joseph. They were completely under his power. He could have given them exactly what they deserved. It would have been justice had Joseph said, "For every year I was Potiphar's slave, you'll be a slave to me. For every year I spent in jail, you'll spend a year in jail. And after you come out of slavery and out of the prison, maybe we'll talk about giving you some food."

But Joseph refused to retaliate, even though he was in a position to do so and, humanly speaking, would have been justified. Joseph forgave his brothers. He realized that getting even was God's business, not his business. "Vengeance is mine; I will repay, saith the Lord" (Rom. 12:19).

The good news is, you don't have to make things work out. God will do that. Refuse to retaliate.

We can learn this lesson by studying the relationships of David to Saul and Absalom.

When Saul was *in authority*, he used his power to mistreat David. He tried to kill him because he saw him as a threat to his throne. When Absalom was *under authority*, he rebelled against David who was in authority.

If you are in authority and don't respond correctly, you are wrong. And if you are under authority and don't respond correctly, you are wrong.

Saul abused power when he had it. Absalom attacked power when he didn't have it. But when David was under Saul's authority, he refused to strike. He had opportunities to kill Saul. He could have justified his behavior because Saul was trying to take his life. He could have rightly claimed it was done in self-defense. Instead, he said, "The LORD forbid that I should do this thing unto my master, the LORD's anointed, to stretch forth mine hand against him" (I Sam. 24:6).

David was saying: "One day God will take care of Saul. But until that day, he is king—maybe not a good king, but king nonetheless. Though he is out to kill me and though I may be jeopardizing my own situation by doing right toward him, he is king. And I will not turn against God's appointed authority."

Later, when the tables were turned and David was king, Absalom rebelled against him. Because God gave him the victory, David was given the chance to crush Absalom and all those who sided with him. Absalom had stolen David's throne and taken David's wives. He had shamed and humiliated David in the sight of all Israel. Yet when David gave his troops their marching orders before the final battle, he said, "Deal gently for my sake with the young man, even with Absalom" (II Sam. 18:5).

Despite Absalom's rebellion, despite his vile behavior, David refused to exact revenge.

Of the three men, only David, both when he was *under authority* and when he was *in authority,* refused to attack and retaliate to get even. I believe that is the reason, in spite of some severe flaws and some terrible sins, that God left David on the throne until an old age.

Please be careful to understand what I am saying. Refusing

to retaliate does not mean that there is never a time to fight. It does not require us to be pacifists. If a man comes up with a gun and says, "I'm going to kill you and your wife," I don't believe that's the time to turn the other cheek. Refusing to retaliate does not mean we should not defend ourselves against physical attacks.

We are talking about injustice, not about matters of safety. If you are in a situation where you are being physically abused or threatened, God does not expect you always to stay and take it. When Saul was trying to kill David, David fled from the palace. God does not expect you to be a doormat who gets abused by everyone who comes by.

Injustice in the context we are talking about is people who are insulting you, mistreating you, being unfair toward you. That's different from actual abuse. There are times when it is right to take action to protect our lives and the lives of others. There are times when it is right to answer an accusation. But there is never a time when it is right to get even.

Remember God's sovereignty. In Genesis 50:20, 21, Joseph said to his brothers:

"But as for you, ye thought evil against me; but God meant it unto good, to bring to pass, as it is this day, to save much people alive.

"Now therefore fear ye not: I will nourish you, and your little ones. And he comforted them, and spake kindly unto them."

Joseph recognized that God was in control of everything that happened.

If we go back to Genesis 45, we see where Joseph had just revealed himself to his brethren. Remember, he was in a position to use his power to get revenge on them. But instead, verse 8 tells us that he said, "It was not you that sent me hither, but God." An incredible statement!

Did God send Joseph to Egypt? Did God sell Joseph to be a slave? Did God send Joseph to jail? Joseph's attitude was that

God *allowed* him to be sold as a slave and be falsely accused in Potiphar's house and be put in jail. And the same God let him be brought out of jail and be named as second in command to Pharaoh.

If we are going to believe that God brought Joseph out of jail and made him second in command of all Egypt, we also have to believe that God put him in prison. Joseph said to his brothers, "Ye thought evil against me; but God meant it unto good." In other words, "It wasn't you who sent me here. I wouldn't have been a slave one day if God hadn't wanted me to be. I wouldn't have spent five minutes in prison if it hadn't been part of the plan of God. As a matter of fact, as I look back now, I can see the hand of God in all of it."

Joseph knew God had placed him in the position he was in so he would be able to help those who had mistreated him.

Everything that happened to him was the result of an act of injustice. It was injustice on the part of his brothers that made him a slave. It was the injustice of Potiphar's wife and her false accusation that put him in prison. It was injustice on the part of the forgetful butler that left Joseph in prison for two years.

But if Joseph hadn't been sold as a slave, he wouldn't have been in Potiphar's house. And if he hadn't been falsely accused, he wouldn't have been in prison. And if he hadn't been in prison, he wouldn't have met the butler through whom he was brought to Pharaoh's attention. It was through Pharaoh that Joseph was promoted. Just as surely as God oversaw all the good things that happened to Joseph, He also oversaw all of the injustice.

I believe one of the greatest truths we can learn to help us deal with the difficulties of life is God has a way of making bad things turn out good. *The worst that your adversary can do to you is be the unwitting instrument of God to accomplish His purpose in your life.*

If you understand the principle of God's sovereignty, your reaction to injustice will change.

People sometimes say to me, "But you don't know what happened to me." After years in the ministry, I probably do know. But even if I don't, even if what happened to you is so hideous and awful and unfair that I can't even imagine it, I still know that God can use it for good.

"Good?" you may say. "The injustice I've suffered has left me broken and unusable." But God took Joseph from prison to a palace. And He is able to do the same for you if you are willing to submit to His sovereignty.

I can't blame God when bad things happen to me or when people do evil things. What we must understand is that God has permitted those things to happen. This is the lesson in the Book of Job. God is in control even if we do not see what He is doing.

The sovereignty of God does not mean that the people who do wrong won't have to answer for it. We've seen enough in the story of Joseph to know that his brothers never got to sleep easy. They never had a clear conscience. They never forgave themselves for the evil they did to Joseph. Nearly forty years after they sold him into slavery, they were still afraid he was going to try to get even with them (Gen. 50:15–21).

But because Joseph knew that God was in control, he had relinquished his claim to the right to retaliate against them. He didn't need to get even because he was willing to let God be God. That is the proper response to injustice.

Rely on God's faithfulness. We talked earlier about the way David responded to injustice. In II Samuel, chapter 16, we find David fleeing from the rebellion of Absalom, when he met a man named Shimei.

David, king of Israel, was running from his own son. And Shimei was cursing David. Shimei was from the tribe of

17

Benjamin, the same tribe from which Saul hailed. Shimei was still holding a grudge against David for replacing Saul on the throne.

Shimei was unjustly accusing David. David had refused to strike against Saul when he had the opportunity. But Shimei was cursing him and delighting in his fall from power. He even picked up stones and threw them at David. Still David refused to allow his soldiers to strike back. He said, "Let him alone, and let him curse."

David decided to rely on God's faithfulness, trusting God would make things come out right.

You don't have to fight back. There have been plenty of times in my ministry when I would have liked to let somebody have it. There have been plenty of times when what I wanted was a big, knock-down-drag-out argument. I've had stones to throw back but decided instead to rely on the faithfulness of God.

A man told a lie about me. I called him on the phone and asked, "Did you say this about me?" He replied, "I don't even know if you are who you say you are." I said, "Well, come to Saginaw. I'll buy your ticket. Talk to me. Talk to my wife. Talk to my staff. Talk to my deacons. Talk to my church." He refused.

After I got off the phone with him, I talked to my lawyer. My lawyer said, "You can sue him and get triple damages under the statute. However much the courts decide he damaged you by that false statement, you get three times that much money."

I even had some good people encourage me to consider suing him. But I didn't—because I have learned that we can always rely on God to be faithful.

Later that day, the man who attacked me talked to his lawyer, who knew the law as well as my lawyer did. Before that, he wouldn't talk to me; after he got through with his lawyer, he wanted to talk! He asked, "What do you want me to do?" I said, "I want you to write a notarized letter of retraction." He said, "I'll do it."

Relying on God's faithfulness doesn't mean that we do not answer accusations made against us. The response I made was, "Come on in. Open the closet. There aren't any skeletons there." Honest people are willing to do that.

There is a reason to answer, but no reason to retaliate. You don't have to get even. You don't have to fight back. You can rely on God to vindicate you when you are right.

Dr. Ed Nelson is one of my heroes. He has been a pastor for decades. One day two pastors, who should have known better, said, "We're going to ruin you." They brought terrible accusations against him. Dr. Nelson said, "I'll tell the truth to anybody who wants to know. I'll answer these false accusations. But I'm going to pastor my church and serve God. My prayer will be, 'Dear God, please take care of those people who are attacking Your servant.'"

Within twelve months, one of those men had a heart attack and died, and the other man was out of the ministry. Ed Nelson is still serving God. At the age of seventy, he started a church in Tucson, Arizona. He still takes trips to Russia and works on mission fields around the world.

I heard him tell this story more than twenty-five years ago. It happened ten or fifteen years before I heard it. God hasn't changed. Rely on His faithfulness. You don't have to fight back. As a matter of fact, when you try to hurt another person, you end up hurting yourself more than him.

ଈଔଔ୬

Jim MacLaren faced a choice that night in Hawaii. Only thirty-three, he didn't want to die, but neither did he want to live as a quadriplegic. That was something he couldn't change, so he decided that night to make peace with what had happened to him.

Jim determined that instead of being afraid of solitude, he would find a way to use it. His classical education led him to read about men who had been wounded. He read about the crippled Greek god Hephaestus. He read about blinded Oedipus. But real comfort did not come until he read the story of Job. In fact, it was the tenth reading through the book before Jim realized God worked through trials and troubles to draw men closer to Him.

Today Jim is working on his doctoral dissertation at the Pacifica Graduate Institute in Santa Barbara, California. He is examining the results of being wounded in body, mind and spirit. People constantly come to him for comfort and counsel. Jim offers them the voice of someone overcoming injustice. He still has fears, but he is learning to face them and go on.

Injustice is a reality in our world. All of us will sometimes have to deal with it. It is not injustice but our response to it that determines the effect it will have on us. If, like Joseph, we respond according to God's principles, we break the cycle of injustice and unlock the flow of His blessings on our lives.

Chapter 2
Overcoming Insecurity

Some years ago I was counseling a lady who had severe problems with insecurity. She told me about one experience. Her husband was to pick her up at the mall. Because he went to the wrong entrance, he was some fifteen minutes late.

By the time he finally arrived, she was in tears. Due to her overwhelming insecurity, she had convinced herself that he had decided to leave her and that she would never see him again.

Most people's insecurity isn't quite that bad. But insecurity is a problem for nearly everyone. Leah is a great example from God's Word of the causes and effects of insecurity. We read this in Genesis 29:15–18:

"And Laban said unto Jacob, Because thou art my brother, shouldest thou therefore serve me for nought? tell me, what shall thy wages be?

"And Laban had two daughters: the name of the elder was Leah, and the name of the younger was Rachel.

"Leah was tender eyed; but Rachel was beautiful and well favoured.

"And Jacob loved Rachel; and said, I will serve thee seven years for Rachel thy younger daughter."

Because he was running from Esau, Jacob had gone to live

with his uncle Laban. His brother was enraged over the deceit that Jacob and his mother had used to trick Isaac into giving Jacob the blessing. In fact, Esau planned to kill Jacob. So Rebekah sent Jacob back to her family for safety.

Jacob fell in love with Laban's younger daughter, Rachel. But after Jacob worked for seven years to pay for her dowry, Laban deceived him and gave him Leah instead. The irony of this story is that Jacob deceived Esau, but then he got taken in by Laban.

Jacob was married to Leah, but he loved Rachel and married her too. That left Leah in a very uncomfortable situation. She knew from the very beginning of her marriage that her husband did not love or want her. She was insecure.

I'm not sure anyone is completely immune to insecurity. Imagine this: when you go in to work tomorrow, a note on your door from your boss reads, "I need to see you in my office right away." What's your first thought? *Oh good! A raise? He must have heard about how hard I've been working.* One's first reaction wouldn't be nearly that positive.

Maybe you go to the doctor for a routine physical. He listens to your heart and goes, "Hmmm." He checks the charts, looks at his notes, shakes his head and then says, "I'd like you to get an EKG and a stress test." You would be at least a little worried.

We respond negatively to things because we're afraid of losing something, maybe our job or our health or even our life. And even if we can handle getting bad news, think what our reaction would be if it were our spouse or child getting bad news.

I. Characteristics of Insecurity

Let's look at four characteristics of insecurity.

The Definition of Insecurity

The definition that I like to use is "worrying about losing what you have." Insecurity is caused by fear—fear of loss.

When we are placing our sense of value or worth in something that we can lose, we are always vulnerable to fear.

Leah drew her sense of security from her husband, Jacob, but she lived with the constant fear that he would abandon her for Rachel. If the source of our security is vulnerable, we can never truly be at peace.

The Description of Insecurity

Insecurity in a relationship is a result of fear that the relationship will be lost. When Leah had her first son, Reuben, she said, "See, I have a son." That is what Reuben means. She felt she had done something that would earn Jacob's love. And since she had done something to satisfy him, she would get the security she needed.

Many people know only conditional love. As children, if they were good, they enjoyed love and acceptance. If they were bad, they felt neither. Some have been reared to feel that if they mess up even once, their chance to know love is gone forever.

The Difficulty of Insecurity

The difficulty is that we allow ourselves to be judged by what we *do* instead of what we *are*. When Leah had her third son, Levi, she thought she had performed well enough to be accepted. Levi means "attachment." She thought Jacob's heart would be hers because of what she had done.

It's what I call the report card syndrome. We feel loved if we measure up. If we make all As, if we have a good job with a good paycheck, if we're successful, we believe we are then worthy of love. But if we have done our best, God is pleased with us regardless of the results.

And by the way, even if we don't do our best, He still loves us. When we sin or fail, we may forfeit some blessings, but *we cannot do anything that will make God love us any more or any less.* It is hard for people to understand this, but it's crucial to enjoying security. We cannot be secure if we do not understand the grace and love of God for us.

The Depression of Insecurity

The depression of insecurity comes from feeling that you must constantly prove yourself—that you are on trial every day. Those trying to prove themselves to gain security tend to be very hard workers, but they're not very pleasant to be around. They are always letting you know all the things they have done and their accomplishments. They are afraid if they mess up just a wee bit, they will lose their standing in your eyes.

Leah kept having children—not because she loved children but because she was desperately trying to perform so that Jacob would love her. She was constantly trying to stay ahead in a competition she could never win.

All of us need to learn how to deal with insecurity in a biblical fashion. To do that, we must find what causes us to feel insecure, then find what God says, and then put our faith in Him.

II. Causes of Insecurity

I believe there are three basic root causes of insecurity.

Parental Rejection

The way in which our parents show or fail to show acceptance reaches into our adult lives in a very real way.

In the Bible account, we find that Leah was pawned off on Jacob by her father. He covered her with a veil so Jacob wouldn't discover the deception until it was too late.

Imagine the effect that had on Leah. She had good evidence that her father wanted her out of his house. Even worse, his opinion of her was so low that he thought she would never be chosen to be a bride. He needed to resort to deceit to find her a husband.

Now the Bible tells us that Leah was not pretty like her sister. She realized that, but how devastating it must have been for her own father to confirm it!

Then Jacob's reaction when he found out whom he had really married reinforced her feelings of insecurity and inadequacy. He didn't want Leah; he wanted Rachel, and he made no effort to hide his feelings. Leah never felt she was good enough for either her father or her husband.

I don't know how many times I've had people sit in my office for counseling and say, "I was always the bad child. I never heard my parents say, 'I love you.' Nothing I did when I was growing up was ever good enough."

Remember, what children think of God is based primarily on the picture their parents give them. What does a child who knows nothing but conditional love and pain think of God? If your parents were abusive or did not show acceptance, it may be hard for you to realize that God will never turn you away.

Pain of Comparison

Leah knew all too well the pain of being compared to her sister and feeling less loved. Kids pick up on differences in treatment. When children constantly hear, "Why aren't you smart like your brother?" or, "Why aren't you as good as your sister?" it makes them feel they must compete for affection and attention. Sometimes a child will try to compete by doing better. But this feeling more often leads to all sorts of bad behavior. In either case, it is very destructive. The child will grow up without the resources to stand alone. He will constantly be looking for the approval and attention he failed to receive as a child.

Since Leah knew her husband loved Rachel more and since her father thought she was ugly, she resorted to the only thing she had over her sister: she could have more children, especially sons. But the damaging thing about this type of competition is that no one ever wins. No matter how many children Leah had, Rachel would always be Jacob's favorite. We can never do enough to gain love and acceptance that lasts.

Possibility of Loss

We're likely to feel insecure when we attach significance to that which can be taken from us. Leah was afraid of losing Jacob. Women in Bible times were treated more like possessions than partners. A woman left alone had no good options except to go home and live with her father, and Leah already knew that Laban didn't want her.

She must have wondered, *What will happen if Jacob kicks me out?* Because he loved Rachel more, Leah was not secure in her position. So she had a son, then a second, a third and a fourth. Her sons were her security against her husband's deciding to send her away.

What do you have that can't be taken away? Health can be lost, no matter how much you exercise and take vitamins. Watch your diet, work out, skip salt, don't use butter, eat lettuce all day—still you might get run over by a truck.

Dr. Curtis Hutson was in superb physical condition. As a young man he was a champion weight lifter who set records in the state of Georgia. He exercised and watched what he ate. But he still got cancer and died when he was in his early sixties.

The truth is, you can't guarantee you will keep anything—spouse, children, job, health, wealth or friends. The only thing you have that cannot be taken from you is your relationship with God. And if that relationship is as important as it should be, everything else is manageable. It's when our relationship with God is not as important as it should be that we struggle with insecurity.

When teaching His disciples, Jesus said, "But seek ye first the kingdom of God, and his righteousness; and all these things shall be added unto you" (Matt. 6:33). The context of that statement is the way the world seeks after the security that comes from things such as food and clothing. Jesus' teaching means our focus should be on God instead of on things. If we do that, we will be secure.

III. Consequences of Insecurity

There are three main ways that insecurity manifests itself.

Intense Drive to Succeed

I talked to a man, a multimillionaire, whose business employs over thirty-five thousand people. He has a full-time captain for his yacht. He has all the toys and pleasures that success in life can offer. Yet his life has been marked by emptiness and a lack of enjoyment.

In our counseling, he told me, "I struggle constantly with low self-esteem. Everything I do, everything I accomplish, is to impress my father. When I was little, he told me, 'You'll never amount to anything.'"

I have a letter from that man telling me how he sat in a motel room with a loaded nine-millimeter handgun in his mouth, ready to end his life because of the emptiness and despair he felt. He said, "I made a million dollars many times over, but I lost something more precious than gold—the love of my youth and my family."

The problem was, his father, who had been dead for years, had never told his son that he loved him or approved of him. There's no way to change the mind of a dead person. No matter how much you accomplish, you can never get love from somebody who is gone.

This man thought if he got the next promotion, the next recognition, the next raise, then he would be acceptable. He kept thinking that one more success would convince his father that he really was worthwhile. But he never got the peace he was seeking.

The intense drive to succeed is a losing battle. No success level or accomplishment will satisfy insecurity because the problem is not a lack of success. Only God can fill the void by offering us His perfect acceptance and love.

Leah felt the pressure to measure up. She believed that if she had babies—sons for her husband—then he would start to love her. So she kept having babies because she was unsure of her value and significance. Leah never learned to separate the failure of an activity and the failure of herself as a person.

So many people have bought into the deception that if they fail at something, they are bad people. Many parents train their children to believe that. These insecure people have great drive. They strive to succeed, but inwardly they remain empty. Unless they learn the truth of God's love, they will never be able to truly enjoy life.

Inadequacy in Relating to Peers

Leah and Rachel didn't get along. There was a constant competition for Jacob's attention. Being insecure made Leah envious and jealous of her sister. It is understandable, based on her childhood and the lack of love she received from her husband, but it is not the right way to respond.

We are not responsible for the way others treat us, but we are responsible for the way we react to that treatment. Leah could have developed a good relationship with Rachel, for they had many things in common, but Leah's insecurity built a wall between them that was never breached.

Over the years I have noticed a pattern in the way insecure folk act toward others. When they are interacting with someone who is above their level, they are usually very polite, even almost subservient. They are also nice to those who are below their level because they don't view those people as a threat.

But when dealing with someone on their own level, they feel a threat. They worry about what that person might take that belongs to them. So they treat those people with suspicion, hostility and unkindness. The very ones who should be a source of friendship and encouragement are seen as a danger.

One of the sad realities for insecure people is that they do not get to enjoy the benefits of having close friends. Insecure people frequently turn others against them. Since they don't think well of themselves, it's hard for them to imagine that anybody else thinks well of them. They are constantly suspicious of ulterior motives. When good things are said about them, they look for hidden meanings. They expect to be mistreated or betrayed.

Some even go so far as to set up situations where people are forced to turn against them. They put their friends, spouses and even children into no-win situations.

Years ago I was counseling a lady who was struggling with insecurity. One day she missed her appointment. I wasn't too worried about it; I just figured something had come up.

She called me that night and said, "You are mad at me, aren't you?" Thankfully, God gave me insight to answer her. If I had said, "Yes," she would have taken that as proof that she wasn't good enough. If I had said, "No," she would have said I didn't care whether or not she got help. She was setting me up.

I said, "No, I'm not mad—just disappointed that you weren't able to come."

She started to react, but then realizing what I had said, she said, "Oh." That is all she said.

She was disappointed she didn't have something about which to be upset with me! Her insecurity led her to look for problems even where they didn't exist.

Inability to Focus on Blessings

Insecure people worry about what they don't have or what they might lose or how they've been mistreated. The result is, they can never enjoy what they do have.

If they get something, it isn't enough. If they lack something, it's an indication of how unfair the world is. If someone says a kind word, they think the person must want something. If a friend doesn't call, it must be because they are mad or upset.

Perpetual discontent is the lot of an insecure person. They are looking for relationships and possessions and achievements and accomplishments to give them some feeling of satisfaction and significance. It never works. No matter what they do, it will never be enough.

We can see that illustrated in the names Leah chose for her first three sons. Reuben means "see, a son"; Simeon means "hearing"; and Levi means "attachment." Leah thought with each son that Jacob's heart would turn to her, but it never happened. We can never achieve our way to security.

And in the process, she did not stop to thank God for the blessings received in having healthy children. Instead, she viewed them as tokens of success in the competition with her sister.

All of us have received many blessings from God. In fact, what we deserve is to be in Hell. The fact that we're not, shows His grace and mercy toward us. Insecurity keeps us from realizing how much we've been given.

IV. Cure for Insecurity

There are four basic steps that comprise the cure for insecurity.

Understand the Purpose of God

He made you just like you are because that is how He wanted

you to be. You have everything you need to be a success in His eyes. Success, Dr. Bob Jones, Sr., wisely said, is finding the will of God and doing it.

Psalm 139 tells us that God begins to work in our lives before we're ever born, shaping us while we're still in our mother's womb. He knows us and has a purpose for our lives. He made us exactly like He wanted us to be. Our parts are fashioned according to His divine plan and purpose. And we are perfect in God's eyes just as we are.

We are born with all the intelligence and physical ability we need to fulfill the will of God. You look just like God needs you to look. You're a *designer original.* You didn't come down an assembly line.

I heard a preacher tell about his son who was interested in being a ventriloquist. Wanting to order a dummy for his son, he called a company that made them. He was told they didn't make any dolls ahead of time. Once the customer specified every detail—hair color, eye color and size—each doll was specially made.

God does the same with us. When we understand that He has fashioned and formed us according to His will, we can conquer feelings of insecurity. It matters not if we're not as tall or thin or handsome as we want to be; we are the way He made us. Our security doesn't lie in those things anyway. Security is in understanding not only that God has a purpose for us, but that He has already equipped us to fulfill that purpose.

Understand the Promise of God

Hebrews 13:5 reads, "Let your conversation [life] be without covetousness; and be content with such things as ye have: for he hath said, I will never leave thee, nor forsake thee." Almighty God, Creator of Heaven and earth, with all power and all wisdom, says, "I will never leave thee, nor forsake thee." No one else can honestly make that claim. But God can make and keep that promise.

We said earlier that we're likely to feel insecure when we attach significance to that which can be taken from us. God can never be taken away from us, and we can never be taken away from Him.

"For I am persuaded, that neither death, nor life, nor angels, nor principalities, nor powers, nor things present, nor things to come,

"Nor height, nor depth, nor any other creature, shall be able to separate us from the love of God, which is in Christ Jesus our Lord."— Rom. 8:38, 39.

Nothing can separate us—you and me—from the love and care of God. Nothing I *can* do will increase or decrease God's love for me. And there is nothing I can *not* do that will increase or decrease God's love for me. The way we live determines blessings, but it does not change God's love.

This was the lesson Jesus was trying to convey to the Pharisees in the parable of the Prodigal Son. The boy had wasted his inheritance and brought shame on his family, but the father was still waiting for the opportunity to welcome him home.

A proper understanding of God's promise never to leave us and the eternal impact that promise can and will have on our lives will help us rest secure in Him.

Understand the Passion of God

If you had been the only person in the entire world, Jesus still would have gone to the cross and died for you. So you are important—not because of who you are but because of what God did for you.

The self-esteem movement, so prevalent in our world, has it all wrong. We are not special because of who we are; we are special because of the price paid to purchase us.

I heard a man say that there are three things people need to know: (1) You are worse than you think you are; (2) God loves you anyway; (3) You can't fix it, but God can. If people understood those three things, it would pretty much put all the psychologists and psychiatrists out of business. Yes, everyone has problems and shortcomings, but God's love and grace can overcome all of them.

God loves you so much—you and you alone—that He allowed His only Son to give His life for you. That is grace, the unmerited, undeserved favor of God. And it is granted to each and every one, if we will just take advantage of the offer. Don't feel that no one loves you or cares whether you live or die. Rest secure in the greatest love the world has ever known—the love of God.

I said earlier that because children form their impression of God from their parents, this can be a difficult truth to understand. If you struggle with insecurity, I challenge you to take a good concordance and look up all the verses in the Bible on God's love. It will take you a while because there are so many. And I'm convinced that by the time you are through, you will have a new appreciation of how much God really loves you. Security comes from realizing and experiencing God's love on a personal basis.

Understand the Provision of God

In II Peter, chapter 1, verses 2 and 3, is a wonderful promise from God:

"Grace and peace be multiplied unto you through the knowledge of God, and of Jesus our Lord,

"According as his divine power hath given unto us all things that pertain unto life and godliness, through the knowledge of him that hath called us to glory and virtue."

Simply put, God has already given us everything we need that has to do with life and godliness. And all these good things come to us simply by knowing God through the Lord Jesus. We don't work or earn or deserve them; we receive them by grace.

Stop and think about that for a moment. I have everything I need. God says so. Insecurity looks at what I don't have and wishes for more; God says I already have everything I need for His purpose. Insecurity says I might run short or run out; God says His supply is inexhaustible.

We saw earlier that God has a plan for us, but He doesn't stop there. He also sees to it that we have everything we need to accomplish that plan. God has committed Himself to supply our needs.

A guarantee from me that your needs would be met wouldn't carry a whole lot of weight. But if Bill Gates called and promised to cover all your bills, you would never need to worry about money again. But how much greater are the resources of God! And He has promised "all things" that we need. No greater security can we possibly have than that! God will supply, so we need not worry or fret or wonder. We need simply to trust in His promise of provision.

There will always be something we can focus on that will be a problem. When Peter was walking on the water, he took his eyes off Jesus. It was when he looked at the wind and the waves that he began to sink. We too will fail if we take our eyes off the promise of God's provision. Don't do that! Rely on God with complete confidence, knowing that He will never fail. If we will depend and rely on Him, we can overcome the painful consequences of insecurity.

Chapter 3
Defeating Discouragement

One of the most dramatic stories in all Scripture is the confrontation between Elijah and the prophets of Baal on Mount Carmel. There the prophet, outnumbered 850 to 1, called down fire from God that burned the sacrifice and turned the people back to God. It was a tremendous victory.

Yet in the very next chapter everything changed. When the report of what had happened to her false prophets reached wicked Queen Jezebel, she was furious.

"And Ahab told Jezebel all that Elijah had done, and withal how he had slain all the prophets with the sword.

"Then Jezebel sent a messenger unto Elijah, saying, So let the gods do to me, and more also, if I make not thy life as the life of one of them by to morrow about this time.

"And when he saw that, he arose, and went for his life, and came to Beer-sheba, which belongeth to Judah, and left his servant there.

"But he himself went a day's journey into the wilderness, and came and sat down under a juniper tree: and he requested for himself that he might die; and said, It is enough; now, O LORD, take away my life; for I am not better than my fathers. "—I Kings 19:1–4.

Elijah went from being literally on top of the mountain to being so discouraged that he was asking to die.

Have you ever been discouraged? Sure. Everyone has. Our children get sick a lot. A new convert starts out well, then back-slides. We run out of money before the end of the month with bills yet unpaid. Perhaps a hero you looked up to and loved turns away from God. Friends of a lifetime turn and stab you in the back.

Sources of disappointment are not hard to find. It's interesting to see that when we break apart the word, we get "discourage," literally meaning "to take away or lose courage." Discouragement means we face life with fear instead of faith, with worry instead of wonder, with cowardice instead of courage.

There's an old story of the Devil selling off his tools. As the people were milling around looking over the goods to be sold, they noticed that the item with the highest price tag wasn't very impressive to look at—an old, somewhat battered wedge. Attached was a sticker with a single word: "Discouragement."

Since the wedge showed signs of wear and heavy use, some-one asked the Devil why this unimpressive item carried such a high price tag. He replied, "If I can drive the wedge of discour-agement between a believer and his Lord, I win the victory every time."

There are causes and a cure for discouragement. Let us learn ways to defeat this powerful tool of our enemy.

I. The Timing of Discouragement

One of the ways to help us overcome discouragement is to recognize when it most often comes.

After a Long Struggle

Discouragement came to Elijah after a long struggle. Three and a half years before the scene on Mount Carmel, Elijah had stood before Ahab and said that because of the king's idolatry, there would be no rain in Israel. After he pronounced that judgment, he had to flee for his life. Ahab wanted to kill him. He blamed Elijah for the drought.

Elijah hid by the brook Cherith and was fed by ravens. But then the brook dried up. God sent Elijah to stay with a widow in Zarephath. The city of Zarephath was in Zidon, Jezebel's home country. There the oil and meal lasted to feed Elijah, the widow and her son. Only after years of struggle did Elijah return to Mount Carmel to face his enemies.

Most things that are right and good do not come easily or quickly. Any long-time efforts—working to make a good marriage, building a Sunday school class, rearing our children, resolving a relationship problem—can lead to discouragement. When we don't see immediate results, we begin to feel like the effort has been wasted. This is when the Devil comes to us and whispers, "Why not just give up?" After a long struggle, we are especially prone to discouragement.

After a Large Victory

Discouragement came to Elijah after a large victory. Mount Carmel was an emotional high point for him. Can you imagine what it would be like to pray and have God answer with fire from Heaven! The altar, the wood, the sacrifice had been drenched with water. The fire burned it all—even the stones of the altar. The people shouted, "The LORD, he is the God"!

Elijah had a great victory. His faithfulness as a prophet of the true God was vindicated, and the false prophets were destroyed. Everything Elijah had been focused on had succeeded dramatically.

It is the nature of life that we can't stay on a peak very long. When we've done a lot and known great success, almost always there's a natural letdown. Often after a high attendance day at church, I feel empty. We have put in endless hours, knocked on countless doors and made phone calls until our ears are sore. Many came, souls were saved, and there was a great victory. But I find myself too spent, too exhausted to really enjoy it.

While we can't prevent that from happening, we do need to be alert and aware of this natural downtime and not allow it to drag us into discouragement.

At a Low Point Physically

Discouragement came to Elijah at a low point physically. After all the effort and energy that he had expended, Elijah was spent, mentally and physically exhausted. We get an idea of how worn out he was by the fact that even though he thought he was running for his life, he lay down and slept. Elijah had no physical resources left.

Famed football coach Vince Lombardi said, "Fatigue makes cowards of us all." Lombardi knew the truth—that it's hard for exhausted people to do what they should do.

It is vitally important that we take care of our bodies. Rest, exercise and proper food are tools that allow us to keep going. It is not spiritual to abuse our bodies and use the excuse that we are doing a work for God.

The great Scottish preacher Robert Murray McCheyne didn't take care of his health and, as a result, died before he was thirty. On his deathbed he told a friend, "God gave me a message to deliver and a horse to ride. Now I've killed the horse and cannot deliver the message."

Physical exhaustion leaves us wide open to discouragement. Jesus told his disciples, "Come ye yourselves apart into a desert place, and rest a while" (Mark 6:31). Let us follow His instruction.

II. The Tools of Discouragement

Let's look at tools used by others to bring discouragement into our lives.

Attack

Jezebel responded to the death of her prophets by threatening Elijah's life. Notice something important. What did Jezebel actually do to try to kill Elijah? Nothing. She just said, "I'm going to take your life." There is reason to believe that this was an empty threat, for there's no Bible record that she ever did anything to follow it up or carry it out. It would have been political suicide to kill Elijah after he had just called down fire from Heaven and killed 850 false prophets. She would have been going against popular opinion. And if she really wanted to kill him, would she have warned him first? That would just make him harder to find. I believe she achieved exactly what she was hoping for when Elijah ran away.

Threats are designed to intimidate. And they only work if you let them. Children use them to get what they want. "If you don't let me do that, I'll run away." I counsel parents to say, "Want to borrow my suitcase?"

If you give people what they want when they use the club of intimidation, they will beat everything out of you that they can. Don't pay ransom—you will just encourage further kidnappings. Don't give in to threats. Many of the attacks that we allow to discourage us are only empty threats.

Alienation

Elijah left his servant at Beersheba and went on alone. When he was most discouraged, who was with him to encourage him? Nobody. Discouraged people often close themselves off from those who could and would help them face their discouragement.

Predators hunt lone animals. The stragglers, the weak, the young—those who are alone are easy prey. There is safety in numbers. The Bible tells us that the Devil is like a roaring lion and he likes to hunt isolated Christians. They are easy targets for his attacks.

The Book of Hebrews tells us not to forsake the assembling of ourselves together. Remember, in the context of the time that book was written, the church was facing great persecution. The temptation was to lay low and not make waves. But God's people need each other most when things are tough.

God doesn't want you to go to church so the pastor can feel good about the attendance numbers and brag at the fellowship meeting. He wants you there "exhorting [encouraging] one another: and so much the more." The church is supposed to be a gospel center, pointing people to the cross. But it is also meant to be a place where believers encourage each other.

Anguish

Elijah prayed to die. He felt sorry for himself. The grief that he felt was deep and painful; the anguish, real. Yet the reality was that Elijah was not being a very good judge of the situation.

He overestimated the seriousness of the problem. In his prayer of distress, he complained about God's prophets being killed. And while some true prophets had been killed in the past, 850 false prophets had been killed the day before— by Elijah.

Sometimes people enjoy their pity party so much that they don't want to be cheered up. They get comfortable with their anguish and don't want to give it up. Elijah was complaining to God just when things had taken a turn for the better. He couldn't even say, "What have you done for me lately?" It had only been one day.

He overestimated the significance of his person. He said, "I, even I only, remain." Many times we feel like no one else is doing anything. It can feel like we are the only ones right with God. But there were seven thousand who had not bowed to

Baal. Elijah didn't have a good handle on his situation. Nothing had happened that justified his wanting to quit serving God. He was willing to let the kingdom of Israel go to the Devil because he was feeling sorry for himself.

I can remember a time early in my ministry when I wondered if I should continue as pastor of the church. The first year we had a Christian school, I had to dismiss a teacher. Because of that, her husband resigned as a deacon. Another staunch member began to doubt the existence of God. Another faithful member became dependent on prescription drugs.

I started thinking that the church had gotten too big for me to handle and that I should move elsewhere and start over.

I called a good friend, Dr. Paul Vandeman, now in Heaven, and told him what was happening. I was not prepared for his response. In a bold, loud tone he said, "It sounds like a normal church to me!"

Don't start feeling that you are the only one left who is doing right and that all depends on you. God always has faithful people who are doing right.

III. The Teaching About Discouragement

When we look at how God responded to Elijah after he became discouraged, we can learn some important lessons that will help us defeat discouragement.

God started the process by giving Elijah food and rest. Then when he got to Mount Horeb, he was ready to learn the lessons God wanted to teach him.

In the Scripture, we find that God asked Elijah the same question twice: "What doest thou here, Elijah?" Both times Elijah answered with the same words of self-pity and defeat. He had been rehearsing his problem over and over in his mind. So when asked twice, he had the same answer.

When we replay problems over and over, they grow. To

41

make matters worse, our negative response to our situation becomes ingrained in our thinking. We are often not willing to listen to counsel or encouragement. We just want to tell people how bad we have it.

If God asks the same question twice, that might be an indication that there is something wrong with our first answer. Elijah's problem was that he was focused on the wrong things. God wanted to get his attention to teach him lessons that would help him refocus on what he needed to do.

Elijah's Position

There are several key words in this question God asked Elijah twice. "What *doest* thou here, Elijah?" God was putting the focus on what Elijah was doing—fretting, fussing and feeling sorry for himself.

For the cause of God, he was doing nothing. He had left the place of service and ministry to which God had called him.

One of the questions I ask people who come to me for counsel because they are discouraged is, "What are you doing for the cause of Christ?" Often the answer is that they have withdrawn from service to the Lord.

"What doest *thou* here, Elijah?" Have you ever seen someone at an airport or a mall walk into the wrong restroom? It very swiftly becomes apparent that they are in a place where they don't belong. There is a quick and embarrassed reaction to being where they're not supposed to be.

God has a place and a purpose for each life. Ephesians 2:10 tells us that before the world was created, He ordained good works for us to do. He wants us to meet the needs of others, to witness for the lost and to show His grace and glory to our world. We are supposed to be people who bring honor to Him.

"What doest thou *here*, Elijah?" God had a place where He wanted Elijah to be. His office was to be the prophet to the northern kingdom of Israel. Yet Elijah had run away, first to the southern kingdom of Judah, then out into the desert.

When you get discouraged, stop and ask yourself, "Did God lead me to this place?" Over the years I've found that discouraged people are almost always out of position. They're living in a place of pity instead of praise; a place of worry instead of work; a place of fear instead of faith.

Sometimes it is God's will for people to physically move. The region where I pastor in Michigan is very depressed economically. Often people leave to find work elsewhere. But sometimes they get down and then give up, when if they would just stay where God put them, they would eventually enjoy the blessings He wants to give.

God's Presence

I would like to have been on Mount Horeb that day when impressive things were happening. A huge whirlwind tore at the very rocks; a massive earthquake rent the mountains; then there was a roaring fire.

While all of that was an impressive display of power, God was not in the whirlwind, the earthquake or the fire. After the fire came a still, small voice—that was how God chose to reveal His presence to Elijah. The lesson Elijah needed to learn was that God is always there. He is always at work. We think if there's no whirlwind, no earthquake, no fire—no visible manifestation of His presence—God isn't really there. Sometimes all there is to our perception is the still, small voice. But God is always there.

When I was a boy, my parents gave me some radish seeds. Now radishes weren't my favorite vegetable, but they had one advantage—they grew fast. You can get a crop of radishes in twenty-one days, one of the shortest growing spans of any vegetable. Yet to a child, even twenty-one days seemed like a long time. Every day I'd check on my plants to see if they were growing. It was hard to tell much difference from one day to the next. Had you watched with me, you might have thought that God's principles of growth had failed. But they were growing.

So often, when there are no immediate results, we say, "This isn't working." Paul told the Galatians, "In due season we shall reap, if we faint not." When we don't see God working in a visible way, some of us conclude He has abandoned us; so we give up.

I remember when time-lapse photography was a new technique. Often it was used to see flowers bloom. By taking pictures at regular intervals, one could actually watch the growing process in what looked like moving pictures.

A lot of the work that God does in your life and my life is so still and so small that the only way we can notice it is to take snapshots. A lot of us are better off than we think. It's easy to forget what it was like a month or a year or ten years ago. God does not always work in big and dramatic ways.

When you climb a mountain with a gradual slope, it doesn't feel like you are progressing very much. But when you get to the top and look back, you see that you have come a long way.

God was telling Elijah, "I am always here." Even when we don't see the dramatic expression of His power, He is there.

Elijah's Power

When the angel fed Elijah, he told him that "the journey is too great for thee." The tasks that God has called us to do exceed our strength, wisdom, knowledge, discernment and answers. The good news is, He does not expect us to do His work in our own strength. We cannot do what God asks us to do without His help. Of course you're going to face things that exceed your abilities—God designed it that way. He wants us to depend on Him.

The journey may be too great for us, but it is never too great for God. He has promised to provide whatever resources we need to accomplish His assignments. He has strength and power to spare available to us. Saying we can't do what we're supposed to do doesn't let us off the hook. The angel didn't tell Elijah to go back because the journey was too great; he told him to eat and gain strength to make it.

IV. The Treatment for Discouragement

There are a number of treatments God offers when discouragement threatens to overwhelm us.

A Godly Peace

To overcome discouragement, God gave Elijah peace. The angel fed Elijah and then let him sleep. He gave him time away from his regular responsibilities to recover.

I know a man who once was pastor of an amazing church. God blessed the work greatly. On his first anniversary, they had one thousand in attendance; on his second anniversary, two thousand. The church was growing and thriving.

But with the growth came problems. He got discouraged and turned in his resignation. Later he told another pastor that God had never again blessed his ministry like He did at that first church. Then he added, "Had the deacons said to me, 'Take a week off; then see if you still want to resign,' I think I would have stayed."

Don't make major life decisions while you are discouraged.

A Godly Provision

Elijah needed food and rest, and that God gave him. He will always give us what we need if we will depend on Him. Seek your provision from God.

When discouraged, we tend to depend more on our own resources. But that's the time we need to rely most on God. One of the benefits of waiting on the Lord to provide for us is that seeing Him meet our needs reminds us that we do not need to be discouraged.

A Godly Perspective

Elijah was not correctly evaluating his situation. God said, "Elijah, you are not quite as big a percentage of the faithful few as you think you are. Instead of being one hundred percent of those who haven't bowed to Baal, you are one out of thousands! There are others just like you. There are people facing problems like yours. They share your convictions and beliefs. There are people who have overcome the difficulties and discouragements you are facing. Their lives are testimony to My faithfulness in difficult times."

It's no coincidence that God sent Elijah to find Elisha. He needed a friend to remind and encourage him that God was faithful. Someone said, "The Lone Ranger wasn't!" He may have been the last of the Rangers, but he always had Tonto with him.

A Godly Project

One of the worst things discouraged people do is withdraw from the service of God. Don't quit what you are doing because you are discouraged. That is the time you need to keep working. God had things for Elijah to do.

Someone said, "Never despair. But if you do, go on in your despair." In other words, don't quit. God wants you to do something for Him that only you can do. And if you refuse to quit, you can accomplish His projects with His power.

A Godly Purpose

God refused to answer Elijah's prayer to die. He told him that there needed to be a judgment. Someone needed to proclaim the truth. There were prophets who needed to be trained to meet the spiritual needs of the next generation. Leaders needed to be appointed over the nations. A replacement for Elijah needed to be selected and trained.

The legendary football coach Bear Bryant, who spent

twenty-five years at Alabama, once told a reporter, "I'd croak in a month if I quit coaching." He announced his retirement at the end of the 1982 football season. He coached his team in the Liberty Bowl on December 29, 1982. On January 26, 1983, Bear Bryant died.

We need a cause, a purpose, a motivation, to keep going. When discouraged, we need to focus on the purpose God has for our lives.

In addition to what God did for Elijah, there was one thing He didn't do. He didn't do a thing about Jezebel. It was long after Elijah had gone to Heaven when she met her judgment at the hands of Jehu.

We think that God is going to deal with the source of our problems. We think God will take away the cause. We think God should remove it. If He doesn't, we think He isn't doing anything. But taking the problem away is not the way He usually works.

God didn't change a thing about Jezebel, but He changed something about Elijah. The problem is not the things you let discourage you; it's the fact that you *let* those things discourage you. When Dr. John R. Rice asked a man how he was doing, and the man replied that he was doing pretty well under the circumstances, Dr. Rice replied, "What are you doing under there?"

Jezebel wasn't the problem. Nothing God did to her would have addressed Elijah's discouragement in the way it needed to be addressed. The problem was Elijah's response to Jezebel. The treatment God gave him—the peace, the provision, the perspective, the project and the purpose—cured his discouragement.

V. The Triumph Over Discouragement

In the story of David in I Samuel, chapter 30, we find three keys to triumphing over discouragement. David and his band

47

of six hundred men who were running from Saul lived in the city of Ziklag, their base of operation.

One day while they were out fighting, the enemy came and stole their families, their possessions and burned the city to the ground. When the men returned, they wept until they had no more power to weep. When the initial grief passed, anger set in. The Bible says that the people spoke of stoning David. If anybody had an excuse to be discouraged, it was David. But he triumphed over discouragement.

David's Recognition

The men had lost their families and their faith in God, and David had lost favor in the eyes of his followers.

It's tempting to try to deal with our problems by refusing to admit they exist. However, when the stones are being sized up for throwing potential, it's time to face the facts. To conquer the problems we face, we must address them as they really are.

David's Response

At first he was greatly distressed—a natural, emotional response. When things go wrong, it is normal to be sad. But David didn't stay wallowing in his discouragement.

His next response was the right response: "David encouraged himself in the LORD his God." All sources to which people normally turn had been taken away, and there was no help for his discouragement anywhere.

He couldn't find encouragement from his followers, for they had turned on him and were even talking about killing him. He couldn't find encouragement from his family because they had been taken from him. He couldn't find encouragement from his house or his possessions because they too had been taken away. There was no encouragement anywhere—except God.

God never changes, never leaves, never stops working,

never abandons us. He will never forsake His children. What looked like utter disaster to David and his men was no problem for God.

To encourage himself in the Lord, David reflected on the ways God had helped him in the past. He could look back at the way He had delivered the lion and the bear into his hands when he was a shepherd. He could remember his encounter with Goliath in the valley of Elah. He could reflect on escaping from Saul time after time. Seeing God working in his life gave him confidence that He could and would see him through even though, humanly speaking, there was no hope.

Never forget, especially when discouraged, what God has done for you in the past.

David's Result

Because they relied on God when they were discouraged, they gained total victory over their enemies and recovered all they had lost. Not one child, one coat, one animal was lost. Nothing was taken that was not restored.

When David found his courage in the Lord and got everything back, that was when everything turned around. Despair and discouragement turned to joy and triumph.

We can depend on God to give us victory when we trust Him. Keep on trusting Him. Keep on staying faithful.

When I came to this church in 1975, we had around fifty people for church on Sunday morning. The budget was $385 a week. The offerings averaged $200 a week. I was excited when I got here. I wanted to reach people for the Lord.

I didn't know what might happen to the local economy. Back then there were some one hundred thousand people in Saginaw; now there are sixty thousand. We don't have a Welcome Wagon anymore; we just have farewell booths to wave at the people who move away.

After a while I started to get discouraged. We didn't have

many people, not much money, and no good buildings. Every time it rained, worms crawled inside to get out of the mud. A man came in to scrape the worms off the floor before Sunday school.

I remember driving by other church buildings in our town and marveling at the size and quality of their facilities. I told the Lord, "Lord, they don't even preach the Gospel. They're letting people go to Hell. Yet they have these beautiful buildings, and we have almost nothing." Now our church property is valued at over $6,000,000. God has blessed us beyond anything we ever dreamed.

It would have been easy to give up, but God sent me some wise counselors to point me to Him. He sent us some wonderful, dedicated people who were following Him. And because we were faithful, God blessed. When we turned to Him for strength and supply, He met our needs. If I had given up in those early days, I would have missed the blessings God had planned for my life.

Discouragement can be defeated when we rely on God instead of our own strength. He meets the challenges that all of us face from time to time. You too can know the triumph David experienced rather than the discouragement Elijah suffered.

Chapter 4
Overcoming Disillusionment

"But when the first came, they supposed that they should have received more; and they likewise received every man a penny.

"And when they had received it, they murmured against the good-man of the house,

"Saying, These last have wrought but one hour, and thou hast made them equal unto us, which have borne the burden and heat of the day.

"But he answered one of them, and said, Friend, I do thee no wrong: didst not thou agree with me for a penny?

"Take that thine is, and go thy way: I will give unto this last, even as unto thee.

"Is it not lawful for me to do what I will with mine own? Is thine eye evil, because I am good?"—Matt. 20:10–15.

She sat across the desk from me. I had known her for a long time, or at least I thought I knew her. As a college student, she got involved in an inappropriate relationship. Her parents were appalled when they found out what she had been saying to a young man.

I asked her parents if there was anything I should know in order to help her, and that's when the rest of the story came out. As a young teenager, she had been terribly taken advantage of by a person in leadership, a spiritual leader she should have been able to trust.

As I tried to help her, it seemed I was getting nowhere. Then the Holy Spirit gave me a moment of insight, and I said, "You're sitting there wondering if I'm the same type man as the one who took advantage of you. When I stand up to preach, you probably wonder what I've done that hasn't yet been found out. You distrust me and your father and every other man in authority, don't you?" She answered, "Yes." She was disillusioned.

The parable Jesus told about the householder and the laborers contains a powerful lesson about disillusionment. The first workers were very disappointed when they should not have been. And from their example we can learn how to handle life when things don't go our way.

The marketplace in Jesus' day was like the unemployment office today. People who didn't have a particular place to work would go there, and the employers would come and hire them for projects.

In Bible times it was typical to work a twelve-hour day, from around six in the morning to six at night. The householder and the workers who were hired at the beginning of the day agreed on a wage of one penny, the going rate for a full day's work.

The householder kept returning to the marketplace throughout the day and hiring additional workers. There was no wage agreed on for those who started later in the day. He just told them, "I'll pay you what is right." He even hired some workers one hour before quitting time.

The custom then was to pay people at the end of every day. The householder started by paying those who had begun working last. And even though a fair day's wage for a full day's labor was one penny, those who worked only one hour received a penny.

Can you imagine the stir that caused when the other workers saw that? The expectations of those who had been working since six o'clock in the morning were raised. They undoubtedly began multiplying the hours they had worked by the new wage and calculating how much more they would receive. They expected more than they had agreed to work for, when they saw what the latecomers received. Then, when the early comers were disillusioned because they received what they had been promised, the householder responded, "Is it not lawful for me to do what I will with mine own?"

This is a great principle to remember when we respond to the way God deals with His servants. He is sovereign. He has the right and authority to do whatever He pleases. Let us be careful not to let God's generosity in giving someone else more than we think they deserve, turn us into evil thinkers. God's goodness should be cause for rejoicing, not complaining.

The primary teaching of this passage is that God will fully reward all of His servants, no matter when they enter into His work. You are not judged as to whether you compare well with somebody else; you are judged by your potential and your opportunity and how well you measure up to that. The standard is what you did with what God gave you.

But there is another application to the parable which deals powerfully with the problem of disillusionment. The men who had agreed to work for a penny were disappointed when they received their agreed-to wage. Why? Because they "supposed that they should have received more." There was no logical reason for them to think that.

The last people hired were paid first. When the first workers saw that the last workers got a penny for working an hour, they thought they would get more. But when they also saw the three-, six-, and nine-hour workers get paid a penny, they should have realized that a penny was going to be the wage for everyone. There was plenty of evidence right in front of their eyes.

To be upset, they had to nurture an illusion. They had to believe something for which there was no logical or legitimate basis in order to imagine they were going to get more than they had been offered. Regardless of the length of time they had worked, everyone who worked that day was receiving exactly the same wage.

I. The Roots of Disillusionment

One of my favorite *Far Side* cartoons featured a field of sheep. Three of the "sheep" were standing up and had removed their sheep's heads. You could see that they were really wolves in sheep's clothing. If you looked carefully at the rest of the flock, you could see a double line around each of their necks, which indicated the rest had a head that would come off too. One of the standing wolves turned to the other two and said, "Wait a minute. Aren't any of us sheep?"

Sometimes we wonder if anybody is for real. We find out bad things about good people. Even if they are not real bad things, they still destroy the image we had built up, that those people were almost perfect. Sometimes we can hardly believe the terrible things they have done. It's not hard to become disillusioned as we look around us.

An Unrealistic Belief About People

There was no reason for any worker to suppose that he should have received more. The man plainly said each would receive a penny. At the end of a day's work, they did receive a penny. The householder did exactly what he said he would do. The only basis for their belief was in their own minds.

Sometimes we have unrealistic beliefs about people. We elevate them in our thinking. We view them as perfect. We think they never make a mistake or do anything wrong. They never exhibit human weakness.

Years ago I hired a man to be our first full-time music director. He had been saved while attending a secular university. After he graduated, he went to a Christian college to prepare for the ministry. When he got there, he was disillusioned. He had been a Christian in a pagan school; now he was looking forward to being a Christian in a Christian school. He expected everybody there would be spiritual. But they weren't. To his amazement he found that although they were in a Christian college, they were just like him. Even the teachers weren't perfect Christians.

After he graduated, he went to work in a church he had attended while in college. When he got on staff, he found out things he didn't know about when just a member.

When he came to work for us, he wanted to replace the flooring in the house he had moved into. I used to do that in college, so I went to help him. He began sharing some of his disappointments in life. Kneeling there on the floor, he looked up at me and said, "You're not going to disappoint me, are you?" I answered, "Of course I will." And, by the way, I kept that promise! If you expect people to be perfect, you are on a collision course with disillusionment.

It's natural for us to look up to people. We hear a preacher who touches our heart, but then we find out he has a fault. I am not excusing people's faults, but when you see flaws in others, remember this: God never said He had perfect followers; He said His followers have a perfect Saviour. Truth is always truth, even if it arrives in vessels made of clay.

An Unrealistic Belief About Provisions

The laborers thought the householder was going to give them more than he had promised.

I was with a pastor in New York a few years ago. He asked

me to go with him to visit a lady who had been very active but who had quit coming to church when she had some disappointments. Here was the source of her distress.

She had entered Publishers Clearinghouse Sweepstakes. She felt like God had promised her she would win the sweepstakes, but she didn't. Then when her cat became sick, she prayed for it, but it died. I could tell immediately she was bitter when she said to the preacher, "God let me down." She thought God would do something He didn't do.

When we become disillusioned, we have really just lost something that wasn't real in the first place.

Sometimes church members make the pastor something he is not. I tell my people not to put me on a pedestal. God is the Source; the pastor is not. It's good to honor the pastor because of his office, but he is not to be worshipped. Over the years I've learned that the people who seem to worship the pastor won't be around very long. The first time something goes wrong, out the door they go.

The disillusionment is not always without cause. Some preachers have fallen into deep sin. A church called me and asked me to come and help them after their pastor fell. One of the men prayed in the meeting, "Father, somebody we love has done something unspeakable." They were devastated. But I pointed them to the Source of provision that never fails.

II. The Results of Disillusionment

Dealing improperly with disillusionment often leads to serious consequences. Let's look at four alarming results of disillusionment.

Universal Condemnation

The psalmist said, "I said in my haste, All men are liars" (Ps. 116:11). When disillusioned, we think everybody is rotten. A pastor who led his church out of the Southern Baptist

Convention in the 1950s went to Dr. John R. Rice for counsel. He was upset with some pastor friends who were still in the Convention. Dr. Rice listened to what he had to say, then asked him, "Are those men wicked?"

"Yes," the pastor replied.

"Are they all wicked?" Dr. Rice asked.

"Yes," he answered.

"How long have you been out of the Convention?"

"Six months," came the reply.

"Were you wicked six months ago?" Dr. Rice asked.

When we are disillusioned, we paint others with a very broad brush. We see only failings everywhere we look.

Unending Conversation

The disappointment a person has suffered is all they can talk about. It fills every conversation. That's a very negative thing because disillusion spreads to others. We see this illustrated in the life of Absalom.

Absalom was disillusioned with David because David did not deal properly with Amnon's sin against Tamar. Then David did not deal properly with Absalom, refusing even to see him. The Bible tells us that Absalom talked to every person who came to see the king for justice (II Sam. 15:2–4). He recounted the lack of justice he had experienced and promised the people that he would do things better if he were in charge. The constant rehearsal of the problem deepened his own disillusionment. But even worse, it spread that disillusionment to others.

Ungodly Contention

Although Absalom had grounds to be disillusioned with David, his failure to deal properly with that disappointment led to a rebellion against authority. Absalom's disillusionment spread so far that it divided the entire nation.

57

He wanted others to be as unhappy as he was. Disillusioned people don't like to see others happy. The problem is, those people who try to get others to be unhappy are helping the Devil. God hates those who sow discord (Prov. 6:19).

Unbelievable Corruption

People who do not deal properly with disillusionment often wind up doing the exact thing that bothered them. Absalom was upset with immoral behavior, yet he followed the ungodly counsel of his friends and went in to his father's concubines.

I knew a man who was greatly bothered when preachers fell into immorality. In fact, the fall of some made him suspicious of all preachers. He would predict that a certain preacher would fall, even writing down the day he made the prediction. And sometimes he would be right. One day that man himself fell into immorality. His disillusionment led him to focus on evil. Eventually that took its toll on him, and he fell to the same sin that had so disgusted him in others.

It's like driving a car. You head in the direction you are looking.

III. The Remedy for Disillusionment

So how can we overcome the inevitable disillusionment all of us face from time to time?

Recognition

Recognize that everyone is made of clay. "For he knoweth our frame; he remembereth that we are dust" (Ps. 103:14). God is grieved when we sin, but not surprised.

Don't be startled when someone fails. As a wise man once said, "The best of men are men at best." Understanding ahead of time that people will let us down prepares us to respond properly when it happens.

Realization

Realize we are capable of the same failing. There is no sin that anyone else has committed that we could not also commit. The Bible tells us that all of us face the same temptations: "There hath no temptation taken you but such as is common to man" (I Cor. 10:13).

Rather than being proud and condemning others, humbly realize that, except for the grace of God, you would be in exactly the same situation.

Rememberance

Remember those who have stayed faithful. At the beginning of the Book of Job, God bragged on Job to the Devil. He wasn't focused on the failures of men; He was thinking about the faithful. We ought to do the same. We are not alone in doing right.

The older I get, the more I appreciate men who have been faithful for a long time. I think about Dr. Lee Roberson, who has been preaching for more than seventy years. He hasn't changed. He has stayed by the stuff. I'm not saying he is perfect. There were things that I'm sure he would change if he could go back and do them again. But no one has ever questioned his faithfulness.

Focus on the ones who have made it in spite of the attacks of the Devil. In spite of having a body of flesh and a sin nature, they stayed true. Praise God for faithfulness!

I don't like it when people get upset and leave my church, but so many more who get upset stay. They write letters, make phone calls and try to get others mad, yet they stay. Normal churches have trouble. There will always be people doing poorly and people doing well. I decided years ago that I would pray for the ones doing poorly and try to encourage them. But I spend most of my time rejoicing in those who are doing well. Your outlook is determined by where you decide to look.

Refocusing

Refocus your attention on Jesus. "Thou wilt keep him in perfect peace, whose mind is stayed on thee: because he trusteth in thee" (Isa. 26:3). When we allow disillusionment to upset us, unsettle us and unnerve us, our minds are not focused on God. When our focus is on Him, we will have peace.

"My soul, wait thou only upon God; for my expectation is from him" (Ps. 62:5). "Looking unto Jesus the author and finisher of our faith" (Heb. 12:2). If you ever find imperfection in Jesus, then you have reason to become disillusioned and give up. But until He lets you down, keep on going by looking at Him. When difficulties of others might discourage you, tell Him, "Jesus, I'm glad You never fail."

I once heard Alex Dunlap preach. He is now in Heaven, but he had a great ministry witnessing to Roman Catholic priests and nuns.

One day a policeman stopped him for speeding. When the officer walked up to the window, he said, "Sir, your bumper sticker is not true." (The bumper sticker read: JESUS NEVER FAILS.) Alex asked the policeman to read it again; then he said, "*Only* Jesus never fails. I'm Alex Dunlap, an imperfect saint." That is all any of us are.

Suppose you went to a track meet at the local high school to see the 100-yard dash. The winner ran the 100 in ten seconds flat, beating the field by a couple of steps. After the race, you went down to meet the winner and saw that he had a wooden leg. What would you say then? Would you be unimpressed and look down on him for having a defect? No. You would be more impressed because of what he had accomplished in spite of the handicap.

I'm not excusing sin in any way. I'm just reminding you that all of us sin and come short, yet God uses us anyway.

Dr. Bob Jones, Sr., said, "God can hit straight licks with

60

crooked sticks." God has only fallible people to use. So our focus is to stay on the unchanging God rather than on those who fail and come short.

Remember, all the good we accomplish is done with a wicked, sinful nature. Rejoice in the triumphs and victories. And be even more impressed as you recall the imperfect people doing it. They look to Jesus to keep from becoming disillusioned and quitting. And you can do the same.

Chapter 5
Rising Above Depression

"I remembered God, and was troubled: I complained, and my spirit was overwhelmed. Selah.

"Thou holdest mine eyes waking: I am so troubled that I cannot speak.

"I have considered the days of old, the years of ancient times.

"I call to remembrance my song in the night: I commune with mine own heart: and my spirit made diligent search.

"Will the Lord cast off for ever? and will he be favourable no more?

"Is his mercy clean gone for ever? doth his promise fail for evermore?

"Hath God forgotten to be gracious? hath he in anger shut up his tender mercies? Selah."—Ps. 77:3–9.

Depression is the subject of many books, tapes, study series and radio programs. Normally though, when depression is talked about, even by Christians, it is done from a psychological rather than a scriptural standpoint. Be careful. All truth comes from God. To the extent that psychiatry and psychology are consistent with the Word of God, they can be helpful. To the extent that they are inconsistent with the Word of God, they are unhelpful. If you go for counseling and they don't give you Bible principles, go somewhere else for advice.

If you want to address your problems successfully, then find a counselor who knows the Bible and uses it. The trouble with many popular authors in Christian circles is that they have added some Bible to their psychology. They are spiritualizing psychology. But the proper approach is not to start from psychology and add Scripture, but to start with the Bible. A counselor may observe things that will help make Bible teaching easier to understand and apply, but everything needs to have a foundation in Scripture.

Some years ago I heard a famous Christian psychologist interviewed on one of America's best-known Christian radio programs. The host asked, "How do you feel about telling a child he shouldn't do something because the Bible says he shouldn't do it?" The psychologist replied, "Well, I have mixed emotions about that. I'm a little nervous about using the Bible as a club to beat people over the head."

That approach tells you a lot about most of the so-called Christian psychologists. They don't have a high opinion of the Bible. Depression, like any other problem, can be dealt with from the Word of God.

I. The Characteristics of Depression

Let's look at a few major characteristics, or symptoms, of depression.

Inability to Sleep

"Thou holdest mine eyes waking" (Ps. 77:4). Having trouble sleeping doesn't necessarily mean that you are depressed, but it is a common problem for depressed people. So worried are they about their problems that they can't go to sleep.

When our church decided to start our Christian school, we needed a new building for our classrooms. We thought the construction would cost between $150,000 and $175,000. The expert builders came in from out of town and drew up their plans. The final bid was $275,000. And it was June!

I went to bed that night and tried to go to sleep on my right side. I kept thinking, *There is no way in the world we can ever pay for that building.* Then I rolled over on my left side and thought, *It's June! We don't have enough time to get the building finished in time to start school this fall.* I rolled back on my right side and thought, *It doesn't matter if you get it built or not; you will go bankrupt trying to pay for it.* I did that until about 3:00 in the morning. Finally I said, "Lord, this wasn't my idea. You led me to start a Christian school. I'll do whatever You say. You don't pay me to worry, so I'm going to sleep."

Everything worked out according to God's plan. A local contractor built the building for $175,000. We started construction on July 19 and occupied the building on September 19! God can solve any problem. But if we are not relying on Him, it is common that a problem will keep us from sleep.

Inarticulate Speech

"I am so troubled that I cannot speak" (Ps. 77:4). Those who are depressed often find it difficult to articulate a problem. Frequently in counseling I'll hear someone say, "I'm not sure I can explain it to you."

A pastor for whom I worked one summer told me about how his marriage started out. His wife had surrendered to be a full-time Christian worker as a girl and had decided never to marry. When they met and fell in love, he wanted to get married, but she wasn't sure that was God's plan for her life. They sought godly counsel and were told it was all right to marry.

They were getting married at a courthouse. She went halfway up the steps and stopped.

He asked, "Do you want to go in?"

"Well, I'm not sure."

"Do you want to go back?"

"Well, I'm not sure."

They stood there for a while, and then finally he said, "We've got to do something."

They went ahead and got married. For the first six months, every night when he came home from work, he found his wife crying. For months he would ask her every night what the trouble was. With tears streaming down her face she would reply, "I don't know."

Sometimes it's hard to find words to express our emotions.

Incorrect Sight

"I have considered the days of old, the years of ancient times" (Ps. 77:5). We see that the psalmist was focused on the "good old days." Things used to be more exciting and enjoyable than they are now. Many times a depressed person will make this comment: "It seems like my life was so much better in days gone by."

The truth is, things weren't all that great in the "good old days." There have always been problems and always will be problems. You can always find something to pull you down. But you can also find things to look forward to. If you are living for God, He has good things for you in the days ahead. The good times aren't gone for good.

Inward Searching

"I commune with mine own heart: and my spirit made diligent search" (Ps. 77:6). Depressed people frequently turn inward and ask counsel of themselves. We search inside to see what is wrong. The Bible has very little positive to say about introspection. We are told to examine ourselves when we take the Lord's Supper and see if we're right with God. But basically the message tells us to focus on God, not on ourselves.

"Looking unto Jesus the author and finisher of our faith" (Heb. 12:2). Looking at ourselves can be very destructive. We can see ourselves doing pretty well and become proud. Or we can see ourselves doing poorly and become depressed. Either view is partly true and partly false. If we look at Jesus, we see we have a long way to go. But we also see that we have a wonderful Saviour to help us on the journey. Depressed people look in the wrong place for answers to their problems.

Inundation of Sorrow

When people are greatly depressed, they can feel inundated with sorrow. "Is his mercy clean gone forever? doth his promise fail for evermore?" (Ps. 77:8). Buried by his burdens, the psalmist felt as if there was no hope for that day or any other day.

Years ago we needed to build a new building at the church. It seemed as if we couldn't get started. The money had been raised, the plans had been drawn, and we had hired a contractor—but nothing was happening. After some weeks I started calling the builder on a regular basis.

One day I got a little abrupt with him: "I drove by the site, and nothing has happened," I said.

"I'm thinking of getting out of this business," he answered in tears. "Nothing goes right. There are always troubles. It's never good."

Not only did he not get out of the business, but his construction company is now a tremendous success; he is worth millions of dollars. But at that point, he felt inundated with sorrow.

"I just can't take it anymore. If I have one more day like today, I think I'll just explode," a depressed person may say. The problems can become so large and so weighty that one reaches the breaking point. The word "depress" literally means "to push down". Our sorrows can become so weighty that the load seems more than we can bear.

The psalmist felt as though his sorrows had mounted so high that he would never be able to be happy again. In the depths of his depression, while he was looking at himself, he saw no hope for the future.

A few years ago some scientists did a series of experiments with rats. In the first experiment rats were put in a tank of water to see how long they could swim. After a benchmark was established, a second set of rats was put in the water. This time, about five minutes before the rats would have drowned, they were rescued.

The scientists dried off the rats, fed them a good meal and let them rest. Then the rats were put back in the tank. They swam almost three times as long as the first set of rats. What was the difference? The rats had hope. When you feel as if you're about to drown, look up. God is there to help.

II. The Causes of Depression

What causes God's children to become depressed? Let's look at a few of the sources of depression.

Having an Indicted Sovereign

"I remembered God, and was troubled" (Ps. 77:3). Are we supposed to be troubled when we remember God? No! Thinking about God should encourage us. Our good, wonderful, merciful God loves us. The psalmist was troubled because he was not viewing God properly.

I visited a man who was in jail for stealing a car. He admitted the theft, but he then told me, "I asked God to give me strength to do right, but He didn't."

I asked him, "What should God have done that day you went out and stole the car?"

He said, "He could have made me sick."

God doesn't work that way. That man had a distorted view of what God wanted to do in his life.

Some people are blaming God. They say things like: "God

killed my wife"; "God took my mother"; "God robbed me of my health"; or "God let me lose my wealth." Remember this: God never does anything evil or wrong.

When the Devil received permission from God to prove Job's faithfulness, all of Job's possessions were destroyed. Remember what one of the servants said when he came to tell Job about the tragedy? "The fire of God is fallen from heaven, and hath burned up the sheep" (Job 1:16). It wasn't God who did that. He only gives what is best for us.

Some people are bitter at God. A thirty-year-old lady's mother died. She became angry at God. Instead of thanking Him for having a wonderful mother for thirty years, she complained about what she had lost. Finally a wise counselor was able to help her with this illustration.

"Suppose someone knocks on your front door tomorrow, and when you open the door, the man standing there gives you $100. He gives you no information, except that he is there to give you the money.

"The same time the next day, the same man is there with another $100. By the third morning, you will be waiting for him with a cup of coffee. This happens every day for thirty days.

"On the thirty-first day you watch him drive up—but instead of coming to your door, he goes to your neighbor's house and gives her $100. Your likely response is, 'Why are you giving her *my* $100?'"

The point of that counselor's story is this: the woman had been given her mother for thirty years, but then she complained when death took her.

God owes you nothing; be grateful for everything He gives you. Only God's grace keeps us out of Hell. No matter what has happened to us, we have no grounds for bitterness toward Him. All that God gives us is a gift. We deserve nothing.

Some people are bothered by God. "I cried unto

God...and he gave ear unto me" (Ps. 77:1). We get upset when God doesn't respond like we think He should.

By the time Jesus got to Bethany, Lazarus had been dead for four days. Sisters Mary and Martha came out to meet Jesus separately. Each said exactly the same thing: "Lord, if thou hadst been here, my brother had not died" (John 11:21,32). Because Jesus didn't deal with the problem in the way they had anticipated, they were upset with Him. But I ask you this: After Lazarus was raised, would they have traded God's way for theirs? Absolutely not.

A godly pastor's daughter began dating a young man her parents did not trust. They warned and cautioned her, but she would not listen. She eventually married the young man. Every prediction they had made came true. He left her alone and brokenhearted, with two children to rear.

A friend asked her parents, "Suppose I were God and could go back and change everything that has happened. Suppose I could erase the pain, the hurt, the scars of your daughter's relationship. Would you want me to do it? But before you answer, remember that if I turn back the clock and erase this relationship, those two beautiful grandchildren you love will also cease to exist."

Even in the midst of heartache and sorrow, there is much about which we can and should rejoice.

God's way will work things out for the best. He is the Sovereign. He is in charge of everything. We must trust Him rather than allow our circumstances to make us lose faith in His goodness and His love to us.

Having an Insistent Self-Pity

"My soul refused to be comforted" (Ps. 77:2). There are real physical problems that can cause depression. But I've learned over the years that some people are depressed because they want to be depressed. They enjoy their pity party and don't want to give it up.

Some won't quit feeling bad until they have convinced everyone around how miserable they are. It's almost as if they enjoy feeling bad.

When I was a boy, my mother believed children should go to bed early. In the summertime, when the days were longer, my friends would come by and ask if I could come out and play. Mother would tell them, "He is already in bed." I can't imagine anything worse she could have said!

One Sunday night after church, my parents had friends over for pizza. To my great disappointment, Mother told me I had to go to bed. I went to my room weeping and wailing. Now Mother never gave in to that kind of thing, but I think she felt sorry that I was missing out on the pizza. She came up to my room and told me it was all right to come down and get some pizza. I wouldn't go. In a few minutes, Dad came in with the same offer. I still refused to go. One of the boys who was close to my age came up and asked me to come down and eat with him. But I ate not one bite of pizza that night. I was enjoying feeling sorry for myself.

Having an Interrogating Spirit

"Will the Lord cast off for ever? and will he be favourable no more?

"Is his mercy clean gone for ever? doth his promise fail for evermore?

"Hath God forgotten to be gracious? hath he in anger shut up his tender mercies?"—Ps. 77:7–9.

In the space of just three verses, the psalmist packed in six questions. The proper response for a Christian in time of trouble is not to interrogate God but to trust Him. Whether or not we understand what is happening, we must walk in faith.

At the end of the Book of Job, Job was found guilty of one thing by Elihu: he had justified himself rather than God. Job's concern was to convince his friends that he was good and didn't deserve what happened to him. Elihu reminded Job that his task wasn't to tell how good he was; it was to tell how good God was.

Faith doesn't ask why. Rather, it accepts what God chooses to give us. If we allow ourselves to question, those doubts can easily lead to depression.

III. The Cure for Depression

This psalm gives us a five-step approach to a cure for depression.

Realize You're to Blame

"This is *my* infirmity" (Ps. 77:10). As long as we're blaming others or God for our problem, there is no way to solve it. We cannot begin to deal with the difficulty until we acknowledge where the problem really is.

A man worked with me at the church a number of years ago. When I gave him instructions that perhaps weren't as clear as they should have been, he would say, "I need you to help me with this." He never threw the blame on me; he just asked for help for himself.

Here is the way we should react: "God, You don't have a problem; the problem is my problem. It may be the way I'm responding, or it may be I'm not exercising faith, or it may be I'm not learning. I want to acknowledge the problem is mine, and I'm asking You for help."

Recall God's Blessing

"I will remember the years of the right hand of the most High" (Ps. 77:10). The right hand is the hand of power, of deliverance, of blessing. It is the hand of strength and salvation. It is the hand that guides us through our difficulties. The psalmist began to rise from his depression when he said,

"I will remember God's wonderful, strong, powerful provision for me."

When we're depressed, we look at God as the God of sorrow, not the God of strength. We say, "This is terrible" instead of saying, "The way You have sustained me and cared for me has been wonderful."

When Samuel was judge over Israel, he set up the Ebenezer stone near the city of Mizpeh to commemorate their victory over the Philistines. Ebenezer means "hitherto hath the LORD helped us" (I Sam. 7:12). We too need to have things in our life to remind us of how good God has been. When you feel hopeless and helpless, recall the blessings, the answered prayers, the many times you have seen God work.

Remember God's Works

"I will remember the works of the LORD" (Ps. 77:11). The focus here is on the public works of God. This is calling to memory all that God has done. Sit down and review what He has done.

Simply by speaking, God created everything in the world. Remembering that, I know He can take care of my little problems.

Hezekiah prayed when the Assyrians besieged Jerusalem, and in one night, a single angel killed 185,000 soldiers to bring deliverance.

When the people shouted on the seventh day, the walls of Jericho fell down flat.

When Pharaoh threatened the Israelites, God opened the Red Sea and they walked through on dry ground.

More than forty references in the Bible refer back to the crossing of the Red Sea. Why is that? So we will remember God's wonders of old. When we pause to reflect on what He has done, it changes how we look at our problems. Compared to the power and might of God, nothing that faces me is insurmountable.

Refocus Your Mind

"I will meditate also of all thy work, and talk of thy doings" (Ps. 77:12). Meditation is one of the key steps in overcoming depression. Chew on the good things God has done for you instead of on your problems. Make it so much a part of your mind that when you speak, it will be natural for words of praise to come forth. What we think about determines our outlook on life.

Where is your focus? Do your problems turn you away from God or toward Him? When we meditate, it brings our attention back to God. As we ruminate on His works and talk of His doings, it changes our attitude toward our problems.

Rejoice in the Lord!

"Thy way, O God, is in the sanctuary: who is so great a God as our God?

"Thou art the God that doest wonders: thou hast declared thy strength among the people.

"Thou hast with thine arm redeemed thy people, the sons of Jacob and Joseph. Selah."—Ps. 77:13–15.

No matter how things look, we always have room for rejoicing. We can rejoice in how good God has been to us. We can rejoice in His power, His goodness, His strength, His redemption. Start praising God for the good things He has done in your life. When we praise the Lord out loud, it has an effect on our spirit.

The psalmist here is recalling the plagues God brought on Egypt to deliver His people. The deliverance from Egypt is a type of salvation. God's people were called out of the world to follow Him to the Promised Land.

The answer to our doubts about God's love, mercy and

Rising Above Depression

goodness is to review His redemption. Remember how God saved you. When you wonder if God loves you, look at Calvary. There the very Son of God shed His blood to pay for your sins. He willingly gave up His life so that you could be part of His family.

The apostle Paul told the Philippian church to "rejoice in the Lord alway" (Phil. 4:4). When we can't find anything else to rejoice in—when everything around us seems hopeless—we can always find our joy in His unchanging love for us.

There is a fascinating phrase in Psalm 77:19: "Thy footsteps are not known." God is frequently at work even when we don't see the footprints. God's power is so complete that often there are no traces left of His work. I'm sure the Egyptians thought the drowning of Pharaoh's army at the Red Sea was just a natural disaster. It seemed to them to be a catastrophe of nature. But it was God showing His power on behalf of His people.

Just because you don't see the evidence of His presence doesn't mean He is not at work. Rejoice in the knowledge that no matter what happens, He will never leave you or forsake you (Heb. 13:5).

Eight years ago John Bishop contracted bacterial meningitis. He lost every bit of his memory. He had to learn to walk, read and speak all over again. As he preaches across the country, he is a tremendous blessing. Always he talks about the goodness of God through times of trouble. Though still in frequent pain, he is always rejoicing.

After one service, a member of the church where he was speaking asked to speak to him. The man's sixteen-year-old son had been killed in an automobile accident. Brother Bishop told me later about their conversation. In still-broken speech, he said this: "I talk Brother Clark. I feel so sorry him. I tell him it not wrong ask God why. Jesus ask God why. Long as you accept God's answers. God's answer to Jesus silence."

I stood in amazement as this man with simple and halting speech shared such a profound truth about accepting the silence of God.

Following the scriptural pattern laid out for us here in Psalm 77 will give you the tools to overcome depression. God's people can and should live in victory over whatever circumstances come. And with His help and power, you can rise above depression.

Chapter 6
Banishing Bitterness

"Looking diligently lest any man fail of the grace of God; lest any root of bitterness springing up trouble you, and thereby many be defiled;

"Lest there be any fornicator, or profane person, as Esau, who for one morsel of meat sold his birthright.

"For ye know how that afterward, when he would have inherited the blessing, he was rejected: for he found no place of repentance, though he sought it carefully with tears."—Heb. 12:15–17.

When I'm counseling people and ask them if they are bitter, most never admit that they are. People don't want to admit it because they know it is wrong to be bitter. Once I was counseling a man who had had some disappointments and problems in his life. I said, "It seems to me that you're a little bitter." He responded, "I am NOT bitter." And he had the scowl to prove it.

We don't like to admit bitterness. I've heard people say, "I'm upset, bothered, disappointed," or, "I'm having a hard time dealing with it." But we can't deal with a problem until we acknowledge it exists. Unless we get to the point where we're willing to face the things that make us bitter, we can never overcome the problem.

Bitterness has been described as a deep dissatisfaction with the circumstances of life. Bitterness is when the sliver of anger, disappointment or disillusionment is allowed to fester and become infected. We allow one or two incidents to set a pattern that affects our entire attitude. Most people at some point in life get at least somewhat bitter. So how should we respond to bitterness?

I. An Explanation of Bitterness

The author of the Book of Hebrews talks about the root of bitterness. That is God's description of bitterness, and it is not an accidental analogy. There are some characteristics of roots that help us understand the danger bitterness poses to our lives and how we can deal with it.

First, you don't see roots from the surface. Bitter people will not usually tell you what is really troubling them without a great deal of examination. Frequently they deny anything is wrong. Sometimes the real cause of the bitterness has been buried for so long that they themselves don't even recognize the cause.

Next, the root of a weed is smaller than the plant it produces. Bitterness may begin over a small incident. But if allowed to remain, it will cause big problems. If we allow the weed to remain, it becomes much more difficult to deal with. It's much easier to pull out small weeds than big ones. Dealing with problems when they arise is much easier than dealing with the effects of bitterness if we do not.

Another thing about roots is, if the whole root is not taken out, the weed comes back and keeps growing. Dealing only with the surface problem, the part that shows, and not allowing God to do a deep work in your life, does little to resolve anything. We must deal with the root problem before things will get better.

Let God be thorough with you. Let God take out the roots. From a distance, a nicely mowed yard filled with weeds and a yard that's all grass look the same. But the truth is, you can't fix a weed problem with a lawnmower. It makes things look better temporarily, but it does not address the cause.

Over the years I've studied people's lives and tried to understand the reasons why they fall. The pattern seems to be that problems are easier to cover when people are young. They can go on in spite of them. But as they get older, more and more things accumulate if they have not allowed God to deal thoroughly with the problems. Eventually they reach the breaking point, and the problem will come out.

It doesn't matter what caused the problem in the beginning; if you don't deal with it, it will grow. So how can we deal with bitterness? We first have to understand where bitterness comes from and what it does to our lives.

The Root of Bitterness

Hebrews 12:15 warns us to be diligent "lest any man fail of the grace of God." There are different kinds of grace talked about in the Bible. One is the saving grace discussed in Ephesians 2:8,9. Some people define grace as unmerited favor. But it is more than that. God gives us good when we deserve bad. Grace is favor when there is a demerit.

Another kind of grace is living grace. Acts 4:33 talks about the early church and says, "Great grace was upon them all." Living grace is when we give good to others even if they deserve bad. This grace fails when we allow ourselves to become bitter.

Jesus told a parable in Matthew 18 of a servant who was forgiven a great debt and who then turned around and refused to forgive a fellow servant who owed him a tiny amount. This is a powerful demonstration of what bitterness does. We are to operate with others on the same principle of forgiveness that God gave to us.

I have counseled people who have suffered almost unbelievable things. They had huge issues to deal with, and I don't for a moment mean to say that it was easy for them to forgive. But we must realize that no one has done as much to us as we did to God. My sins and your sins put Jesus on the cross. If we can be forgiven for that, we can and must forgive others.

The Results of Bitterness

Hebrews 12:15 says, "Lest any root of bitterness springing up trouble you, and thereby many be defiled." I sometimes hear people say we shouldn't be bitter because bitterness defiles us. But the Scripture says "many be defiled." Bitterness reaches out and touches other lives besides your own.

The first result of bitterness is that you are troubled. The person holding the bitterness is the one troubled. The person you're mad at isn't the one who is bothered. Allowing yourself to become bitter about something is like hitting yourself to get even with someone else for hitting you. Not a very smart way to react, is it?

Bitterness that is not dealt with does not go away. We can ignore it, act like it never happened, say that we've moved on, but if we do not deal with it, it will return again and again to cause us trouble.

The second result of bitterness is that others are tainted. This passage uses the illustration of Esau, who was defiled not by his own bitterness but by the bitterness of others. The promise God made to Rebekah before her sons were born, that Jacob would get the blessing, was delayed. The delay made Rebekah angry and bitter. She stepped in to keep her favorite son from being cut out. She took matters into her own hands. Her bitterness actually defiled both of her sons. Jacob became a deceiver, and Esau became profane. Because He keeps His promises, God would have given the blessing to Jacob, but Rebekah wasn't willing to wait on Him.

Bitterness affects us, our family members, our church members, and those with whom we work. Bitterness bothers not only you, it bothers others as well. There is no way to avoid that consequence unless we deal with the problem that caused the bitterness in the first place.

The Remedies for Bitterness

The best thing to do with problems is deal properly with them when they arise. But if there is bitterness in your life, God gives you a corrective remedy.

I counseled a lady some time ago who had been through some awful things. She asked me why some people seem to be able to put the same kind of things behind them and go on. My answer was, "It is not the problem or the circumstance but the person's reaction to it that determines what effect the situation has on him. Those who get over it react differently than those who allow it to make them bitter."

To recover from bitterness, we must forgive. Jesus said if we don't forgive others, God won't forgive us (Matt. 6:15). We forgive others not just *because* God forgave us, but in the same way or manner He forgives. This is the point of Ephesians 4:32: "Forgiving one another, even *as* God for Christ's sake hath forgiven you." It does not say we forgive *since* God forgave us.

To forgive in the same manner as God forgives us, we need to understand His forgiveness. He forgives immediately, the moment we ask, and completely. He doesn't hold anything back to use against us later if we do it again. He forgives permanently. He never brings it up again. He remembers our sins no more.

That is the pattern to follow when we are wronged. But there is no way to forgive like God forgives apart from His grace.

To recover from bitterness, we must also forego. If you really forgive someone for what he did, it's done. The matter is settled. You don't talk about it or think about it or dwell on it. Forgiveness doesn't mean you allow a wrong to continue. If a grandparent molests a grandchild and asks forgiveness, you forgive. But forgiveness doesn't mean you ever let them be around that person again. It does mean you don't continue to dwell on it and try to get even.

Dr. Clarence Sexton has a great definition of forgiveness: "Forgiveness is releasing your right of retaliation." When you forgive, you are not saying what happened was right nor that you don't deserve to have vengeance. You are saying that you have given up your claim to getting even, that you are trusting God to handle it.

When someone does you wrong, there are two proper responses. You can choose not to take offense, or you can deal with the offense biblically. But don't hang on to it, don't nurture it, and don't feel sorry for yourself. That is the path to bitterness. If you find yourself reviewing it over and over in your mind and wanting to talk about it all the time, that is a good indication that you haven't dealt with the situation properly.

Every time you talk to some people, they tell you about something terrible that happened to them years ago. A young man I know is now a youth pastor at a good church out west. His parents moved their family to a specific town so they could put their kids in a certain Christian school. When this young man was in high school, that Christian school expelled him. Whether the action was justified is not for me to say. But the way his family reacted to it made all the difference. His dad said, "We're not going to leave the church or get bitter." They home-schooled him until he was allowed to go back to the Christian school. His father had the right idea: God can override the errors of men. That attitude kept his son from becoming bitter, and now he is serving the Lord.

The wrong reaction could have driven him out of church and away from God. That young man is on the staff at that same church today.

If a man does wrong, he has to answer to God. Don't try to force him to answer to you. God won't let someone else mess up your life unless you allow it to happen. Potiphar's wife did wrong, but God used her wrongdoing to position Joseph for great blessings. Joseph's brothers did wrong, but God over-rode their sin. Joseph's correct response allowed him to receive and distribute great blessings to others. It is our response to offenses rather than the offences themselves that determine whether we let bitterness take root.

II. An Example of Bitterness

The Book of Ruth tells the story of Naomi and her family. They went to Moab, where they should not have gone. They didn't fully trust God to take care of them during the famine in Bethlehem. In Moab, both of Naomi's sons married ungodly women. After some time had passed, her husband and both sons died.

At that point, Naomi decided to go back home. When she returned to Bethlehem, she told the people to call her "Mara," which means "bitter." She said nothing pleasant was left in her life. She felt God had dealt very bitterly with her. In Naomi, we see a clear illustration of both the effects of and cure for bitterness.

Bitterness Blooming

Many bad things happened to Naomi. She had experienced tragedy, disappointment and death. But that was not the reason she was bitter. She was bitter because of her reactions to what had happened to her.

Naomi was unsatisfied. The place He had for her was Bethlehem, but there came a famine in the land, and God's place wasn't living up to her expectations. Even good places have problems. But if we focus on the problems, we don't see God's goodness to us. Because she focused on the negative, she left the place where God wanted her to be.

Colossians 3:19 states, "Husbands, love your wives, and be not bitter against them." I tell the men in my church, "The woman you married isn't perfect, but that is true also of her husband!" Be careful not to focus only on the problems and irritations. That's dangerous in a marriage. Not being satisfied is a symptom of bitterness. It shows we believe we deserve better than the husband or wife whom God has seen fit to give us.

Naomi was unsettled. She left her home, family and the people who loved God. We live in a very unsettled culture. Statistics show that twenty percent of the population of the United States moves each year. We're anxiously looking for the next car, the next job, the next house. If we can find something a little better, then we will be satisfied—we think.

Some people are always looking. They often move. They are looking for a place where things are perfect. I have news for you! There is no such place. Some people move from church to church. Every time something doesn't go their way, they move on. Bitterness makes us unsettled.

Naomi was unfortunate. When they got to the "better place," her husband and both boys died. Then she wanted to go back home.

Bad things did happen. Disasters and difficulties came. Many times when we go away from God's plan, our lives become difficult. Why? God's chastening hand is trying to bring us back to Him.

Bitterness over what had happened to her became the dominating circumstance of Naomi's life. Her daughters-in-law offered to return to Bethlehem with her. These heathen girls were willing to go to a place where they could learn about the true God. And she told them no! She was perfectly willing to leave them behind without them ever knowing about God. Her focus was on all the bad things that had happened to her.

Naomi was unhelpful. She sent Orpah back to Moab. She tried to send Ruth back, but Ruth refused. When Naomi got back to Bethlehem and her old friends tried to talk to her, she didn't want help because she was enjoying her bitterness.

Not only did she not want help, but she was unwilling to help anyone else. Sometimes God's people allow bitterness to make them so disenchanted with God and with other Christians that, instead of drawing people to Christ and His church, they push them away.

Naomi was unholy. She told the people of Bethlehem that "the Almighty hath dealt very bitterly with me." She accused God of acting unjustly. Naomi was judging God based on the painful experiences she had suffered. She didn't stop to consider that God might have had a larger plan. She didn't consider that the bad things might be her own fault because she left the place God had for her.

Some churches do a responsive reading. The pastor will say, "God is good." The people will answer, "All the time." That is a great truth we need to remember. We may not always understand His working nor see a positive purpose in what happens to us, but God is always good.

Naomi was unhappy. When she returned to Bethlehem, the people were shocked to see her. They couldn't believe it was Naomi. Her countenance and spirit had changed. They said, "This doesn't look like the lady we used to know." Her unhappiness was revealed in her countenance.

I said earlier that people who are bitter frequently do not want to admit they are bitter. However, it tends to come out. The bitterness shows on their faces and in their words. They find it difficult to enjoy anything. The things that have not been dealt with grow to overwhelming proportions, drowning out everything else.

Naomi was unrealistic. On her return, she said, "I went out full, and the LORD hath brought me home again empty." But there's a problem with that statement. Naomi went out from Bethlehem because of a famine. She had not been willing to trust in the provision of God, so she had taken matters into her own hands. But now all of that was forgotten.

Bitter people tend not to remember the past accurately. They forget their part in the problems they have experienced. While they do have real pains and hurts to deal with, they often exaggerate what happened. In their mind they have mulled over it so much that the way they remember it seems as true as if it had actually happened.

Naomi was unappreciative. She said she came home empty, but in truth she was not alone. Ruth was with her. Her bitterness led her to value incorrectly the sacrifice Ruth was making for her. She had left family, friends and country to go to Israel with Naomi, yet Naomi said, 'I'm empty' while Ruth was standing right beside her.

So focused was Naomi on what she had lost that she did not appreciate what she had. She downplayed Ruth's value and the importance of her commitment. Bitter people do not appreciate things like they should because they are consumed with the mistreatment and unfairness they have experienced and the things that didn't go their way.

But Naomi's story had a happy ending.

Bitterness Banished

The first step in overcoming bitterness was repentance. To repent means to change your mind. Naomi's repentance began when she decided that she should return to Bethlehem. At that point, she had not overcome the effects of bitterness, but she had changed her mind about where she needed to be.

She came to realize that Bethlehem (where God wanted her) was better than Moab.

Anytime someone has a problem, no matter what caused the problem, the first step toward getting right is a mental step. The Bible says that the Prodigal Son "came to himself." He was still in the pigpen when he decided to change. He hadn't wanted to be in his father's house, but eventually he came to the point where he realized all he had given up and realized it was time for a change.

The next step in overcoming bitterness was a return. It's not enough just to change your mind; you also have to change your actions. Merely acknowledging doing wrong isn't enough; you have to also turn around and do right. Some people say they have repented of their bitterness, but there is no change in their actions. That kind of repentance does not cure bitterness.

We cannot simply bury the past. If unresolved issues are causing bitterness, they must be dealt with. This can be very difficult, even painful, but it is a vitally important step on the road to recovery from bitterness.

The last step in overcoming bitterness was a refocusing. Naomi reached the point where she no longer looked at what she had lost or how she felt she had been unfairly treated. Now she was looking at Boaz. As the kinsman-redeemer, he was a type of Jesus.

While Naomi was focused on the heartaches, disappointments, losses and pain she had experienced, she was gripped by bitterness. But everything changed when she focused on her kinsman-redeemer. She realized that his interest in Ruth could replace what she had lost.

Jesus purchased redemption for us on the cross. He paid for all that we had lost with the fall of Adam. Bitterness is banished when we stop looking at our troubles and start looking to Jesus. He is the only solution to dealing with the very real problems and pains that come our way. We must focus on Him rather than our problems. Only then can we enjoy the freedom from the past that allows us to live fully and happily in the present.

Chapter 7
Responding to Ruptured Relationships

"And the evil spirit from the LORD was upon Saul, as he sat in his house with his javelin in his hand: and David played with his hand.

"And Saul sought to smite David even to the wall with the javelin; but he slipped away out of Saul's presence, and he smote the javelin into the wall: and David fled, and escaped that night."—I Sam. 19:9,10.

David did nothing to attack Saul. He didn't speak of him critically, nor was he disloyal. He never used the goodwill of the nation to advance his claim to the throne of Israel. Rather, he always honored Saul's position. David even refused to harm Saul when he had the opportunity. In spite of that, the relationship between Saul and David was damaged beyond repair. In his jealousy and rebellion against God, Saul attempted to kill David with a javelin at least twice and perhaps three times. Saul was an implacable enemy, bent on David's destruction.

All of us have people who used to be our friends but now are not. Maybe they are angry over an inheritance and the disposal of some assets. Maybe a business deal went wrong. Maybe there was a real or even imagined slight years ago. Now the relationship is broken.

Some won't attend a family function if they find that

certain other relatives are to be there. Their attitude is, "I will never face, speak to or be with that person again."

Why does that happen? Why do lifelong friends stop speaking? Why will family members not be in the same room? And what should we do when that happens? From the story of David and Saul, we can draw principles that will help us properly respond to ruptured relationships.

I. The Roots of Ruptured Relationships

There are three basic roots of ruptured relationships.

Some Relationships Are Broken by Sin

Sin destroyed Saul and David's relationship. First Samuel 18 tells of the women of Israel singing the praises of Israel's great warriors. When those women praised David more than Saul, jealousy began to grow in Saul's heart. He had enjoyed the part of the song about his slaying thousands, but when they sang that David had slain ten thousands, he became angry.

My brother-in-law is pastor of the Community Baptist Church across town from my church. I recommended him to that church more than twenty-five years ago. Recently he reminded me of some things I had told him when they called him as their pastor.

"At first, the other pastors will be nice and welcome you. But as your church begins to grow, they will compare areas where they still have an advantage. After your church passes theirs in all areas, they will quit talking to you."

The sin of jealousy often breaks relationships.

David didn't write the music the women were singing. He wasn't campaigning to replace Saul. But Saul, feeling insecure, was worried about maintaining his power, prestige and place in the kingdom. Thus, he assumed that David was out to take the throne from him. It bothered him to see anybody else receiving praise. He wanted it all for himself.

90

The Bible says, "Saul eyed David from that day and forward." The green-eyed monster of jealousy inhabited his mind and spirit. Every word of praise or favorable comment about David and every good thing that David did made Saul more unhappy. Sin destroyed what had once been a good relationship.

Some Relationships Are Broken by a Stand

In Acts 15 is the story of Paul and Barnabas's disagreement over whether to take Mark on their second missionary trip. They were ready to go back and visit the churches they had planted. Paul and Barnabas had a great relationship. Barnabas had played a key role in seeing that Paul was accepted by the church after his salvation. They had worked together in the church at Antioch, and they had seen great victories on their first mission trip.

Barnabas wanted Mark on that second trip, but Paul didn't want him because Mark had left them on the first trip. The contention between Paul and Barnabas was so great that they couldn't work together any longer.

I believe we can make a case that neither of them was completely right. Barnabas made a decision to take Mark without considering how Paul would feel about it. Paul was adamantly against taking Mark, refusing to consider that Mark might have grown. (It's interesting that later he called Mark profitable and even asked to see him before he was martyred.) Each thought he was right and the other wrong. Neither was willing to give in; so because of their stand on an issue that probably could have been resolved, the first great missionary partnership that had been so marvelously effective was now broken.

If a relationship is broken because you take a stand on an issue important enough to draw a firm line on, then be willing to do that.

I was on a committee one time. I thought what they were trying to do was good, and I wanted to be a part of their efforts. But one of the men told me I should let them tell me for whom I should not preach.

I'm an "independent" Baptist. The word *independent* is not just an adjective that describes my denomination; it's an adjective that describes my behavior. I must be independent of the control of men if I am going to be dependent on and obedient to God. I told the committee members that they had crossed the line and that I would no longer be a part of that group. I was not discouraged or upset. Some men on that committee are still mad at me, but I took that stand because it was important.

Don't regret if what you did caused a broken relationship, if the issue warranted taking a firm stand.

Some Relationships Are Broken by Sanctification

Sometimes in a relationship, one person may grow so much in his spiritual life that the other person doesn't enjoy being around him anymore. The two may no longer have the same interests; they no longer want to talk about the same things. They don't have enough in common to maintain the friendship.

It's not a whole lot of fun to spend time with someone who doesn't enjoy the same things you enjoy. So it is possible that as you become closer to the Lord, some relationships that used to be close may fall by the wayside. That doesn't mean you act like a Pharisee and look down on them; it's just a natural consequence of the sanctification process.

That's part of what happened in the relationship between Abraham and Lot. As Abraham grew closer and closer to God, he didn't have as much in common with Lot as he had before. Since Lot was more interested in the things of the world, they lost the foundation for a solid relationship.

II. The Response to Ruptured Relationships

There are a number of principles I use in counseling those who are having to deal with a ruptured relationship.

The Preservation to Seek

Do not be the one to sever the relationship. A pastor friend of mine had to resign from his church some time ago because of inappropriate behavior. I've called him several times. When he didn't return my calls, I went and visited him. I asked if I could help him in any way. I don't think he will ever ask for my help, but I'm not going to sever the relationship. I wouldn't ask him to preach for me, but I would like to help him. If our relationship is never the same, it won't be because I gave up on him.

Repeatedly Saul tried to kill David, but David refused to respond in kind. In fact, when he became king, David looked for someone in the family of Saul to whom he could show kindness. He was not willing to sever that relationship despite all the problems he had experienced. Do everything possible to make it easy for people to come back into a relationship with you.

Have you ever heard a teenager talk about "breaking up"? I don't believe teenagers should be going together in the first place. But if they do start dating and then break up, almost always each will tell you he/she broke off the relationship. Something in our pride and ego makes us want to be the one who ends a relationship.

But God doesn't want it that way. David did all that he could for as long as he could to maintain a good relationship with Saul.

The Process to Follow

Go through the Bible process before the relationship is

severed. You have two right choices when someone wrongs you. Number one: Choose not to take offense. "Great peace have they which love thy law: and nothing shall offend them" (Ps. 119:165).

Some people are really good at causing offense, but we have the option of not getting offended. If you choose not to take offense, then you don't go around telling everybody about what the other person said or did. To do that shows that you have taken offense. We talk about things that bother us.

The second choice: Do everything you can to resolve the problem and restore the relationship. That responsibility is ours, no matter where the problem lies.

In Matthew 5, Jesus said if we *have* offended someone, go to him. In Matthew 18, He said that if we *are* offended, go to the person who offended us. In other words, whether we are the offender or the offended, we are to take the initiative in making things right.

So many times we adopt an attitude that we are going to wait until the other person comes to us. But it is our job to do everything we can, if we follow the Bible process, to make things right.

This is so important that Jesus said we are to leave our gift at the altar rather than try to worship with a ruptured relationship unresolved.

I once had a difficult conversation, and I was irritated about it. But after thinking about it, I decided that the right thing to do was to let it go. I called the man on the phone the next day and asked if I had offended him or if there was something I needed to make right. Then I told him, "I do not choose to take offense at anything you said."

The Bible process for trying to resolve a problem is found in Matthew 18. We are to start by going to the person alone. We do not go around telling others about the problem. If going alone doesn't work, then we try again with other mature Christians. The point is, we do our best to solve the problem.

The Profit to Remember

Remember the good the relationship produced. One of my friends was very close to another pastor. They had traveled and preached together. Their families often did things together. But then something went wrong in the relationship. My friend didn't go around telling people what happened between them. Every time someone brought up the other name, he would say, "He knows the Bible. We had a lot of good times together. He's a good preacher." He remained focused on the good things that came out of their relationship.

David benefited greatly by his relationship with Saul. Because of Saul, David got to kill Goliath. Because of Saul, David met Jonathan. By watching Saul, David had opportunities to observe and learn how to govern. There were good things on which David could focus.

Focusing on the good that the relationship has produced is not just for relationships that are damaged beyond repair; it helps overcome the differences that everybody has from time to time. This kind of attitude helps keep a healthy relationship.

When the husband of a lady in the church had a bad reaction to the medication he had to take, he became very bitter and critical. Someone asked her how she was able to stay with him. "I remember the good times," she said. Eventually he was able to get off the medication, and things got much better in their relationship.

Don't allow yourself to become bitter toward those who have helped you in the past. Even if things change and you can no longer be close to them, don't hate them or wish evil against them. It doesn't help the cause of Christ if their lives are damaged.

The Parties to Spare

Do not involve innocent parties in the dispute. We see this clearly demonstrated in the story of David and Saul. Jonathan was both Saul's son and David's friend. David did not try to get him to rebel against his father. Jonathan warned David of the danger David was in, but he stayed with his dad. He remained both a good son and a good friend.

I've seen this process repeated over and over. A movement will be blessed by God and will attract a large number of followers. After a while, instead of using the power of influence, example and prayer, the leaders begin using power. They call people and inquire as to their connections. They try to force them not to speak for others. Don't allow others to drag you into their disputes and make you choose sides to be "in" with them.

Good people will allow you the room to make your own decision. Manipulative and controlling people will try to force you to decide in their favor. When you are involved in a disagreement or a dispute, work at keeping it between you and the other person only.

I see this issue frequently with divorced couples. The tendency is to play tug-of-war with the kids. Don't drag your children into a fight with your spouse. Parents talk about how bad the other partner is and give the kids more whipped cream on their hot fudge sundae. Such actions are not only ungodly, but hurtful to your children.

The Position to Respect

Respect the position even when you cannot respect the person. Saul was not worthy of respect because of his behavior. He was selfish and jealous. He devoted an incredible amount of resources in trying to find David to kill him. But Saul was still the king.

In I Samuel, chapter 26, we see what David did when he

had the opportunity to take revenge for all that Saul had done to him. Abishai wanted to kill Saul. David said, "Destroy him not: for who can stretch forth his hand against the LORD'S anointed, and be guiltless?" (vs. 9).

Why didn't David allow Abishai to kill Saul? It wasn't because he was afraid of Saul, nor because he loved Saul, nor because he was wrong and Saul was right. It was because Saul was anointed of God. David realized that God had put Saul on the throne and it wasn't his place to take him off that throne.

I don't believe David respected Saul as a person. He didn't want to be around him or have fellowship with him. He didn't think he was a great leader. But he respected his position.

If your dispute involves someone in a leadership position, pray for him and ask God to guide him. When you talk to him or about him, do so with respect for the position he holds.

The Precaution to Heed

Be careful to whose advice you listen. When you're involved in a ruptured relationship, there are almost always people like Abishai around who will advise you to get even. This seems to be especially true when the relationship involves someone in authority. Anyone who tried to get you to turn against a God-ordained authority in your life is not your friend.

Sometimes people encourage us to do wrong by sympathizing with us when we don't deserve it. That is how Absalom turned the hearts of the nation of Israel against David. He told everyone who came for justice, "Thy matters are good and right." Never encourage anyone to rebel. Direct them to submit to authority unless obedience to the authority requires disobedience to God. And don't take a person's advice just because he is telling you what you want to hear. Most of those people are liars. They talk a good game: "I'd do this or that," but when faced with the same situation, they rarely do what they boast about and advise you to do. If you follow the advice of a person like that, you will end up worse off than you started out.

Those people who are so quick to offer you their advice are usually not around to pick up the pieces after the explosion comes from following it. Make sure that the ones giving you advice are godly people who are using the Bible. Be very careful about whose advice you take about ruptured relationships.

The Priorities to Maintain

Do not overestimate the importance of any relationship. A preacher friend was between churches and needing a job. I called a man in our church who owned a business and asked if he was hiring. He said, "No. In fact, we just lost all our General Motors business." (General Motors accounted for the majority of his sales.)

I said, "That's terrible."

He replied, "Well, we're doing things to try to make it up. But the Lord will take care of us. He always has."

Happy is the businessman who realizes that his business is in God's hands. That man wasn't depending on General Motors but on God.

It's wrong to be ungrateful to people who have helped you, but you must realize that the relationship you're struggling with is not the source of your supply.

A man who worked for me was asked what kind of man I was. He answered, "My pastor is gracious to all and committed to few."

Many get so deeply committed to a person or movement that they cannot stand on their own. If that person or movement falls, down they go too.

One great danger lifeguards are warned about is that posed by a drowning person. In his panic and terror, it is not uncommon for the one drowning to pull the one rescuing under, drowning both. Many allow themselves to be pulled under when someone else goes down.

Don't let another's problem become your problem. The relationship you are struggling with is not vital. People are important, but only God is necessary. David didn't need Saul. God was able to place David on the throne in His own time without anyone's help.

Many years ago my father helped build a new building for the Detroit City Rescue Mission. Some objected to the location of the mission. One man who owned a hotel in that neighborhood objected to it very strongly. My father told him, "If God wants the mission there, it will go there. If He doesn't, it won't. It has nothing to do with you or me."

That businessman later got saved and became a professor at a Christian college. He said later that the statement my dad made that day made a huge impression on him.

Nobody can keep you from the will of God except you. Others can hurt you, make you sad, discourage you and be a bump in the road. They can cause you discomfort, but they cannot keep you from God's will unless you let them.

Some don't go to church because another person hurt them, offended them, mistreated them, did them wrong. My question is, "So what?" By that, I don't mean, "Who cares?" I'm genuinely sorry for the hurt. But what does that have to do with their relationship to God? Why does that keep them from reading the Bible? What does that have to do with their serving God?

If you allow the failure of a relationship to take you away from God, you have placed too high a value on that relationship.

III. Restoring Ruptured Relationships

There are two crucial steps you can take as you strive to restore a broken relationship.

Seek the Possibility of Reconciliation

You always ought to want things to be made right if it's at all possible. Paul said, "If it be possible, as much as lieth in you, live peaceably with all men" (Rom. 12:18). With everything in us, we ought to work toward reconciliation. Deal with the problems in such a way that you are leaving the door open and building a bridge for people to come back.

I don't like it when people leave my church. And sometimes that does happen. But whether or not I think they have a valid reason for leaving, no one leaves the church because I kicked them out. Why not? First, because I need to stay right with God myself; second, I want to do everything I can to make sure they do not turn away from God because of the way they have been treated; and third, they often come back. That would never happen if the door weren't left open.

The truth is, much of the time relationships that could be restored are not restored. We either don't want a restoration, or we at least tell ourselves that we don't. Too often we allow pride and hurt feelings to keep us from doing what we know we should do to make things right. A ruptured relationship will never be restored unless we really want things to be made better.

Stay on the Path of Reconciliation

When a relationship has been ruptured, put yourself in a position that makes it easy for the other person to come back. Make sure your actions convey the message that reconciliation is welcome.

A friend of mine in college married the wrong girl. She turned him completely against his parents. He met with his mother and father and told them that, as far as he was concerned, they didn't exist. He said, "Don't send us any cards or letters. We won't open them. Don't call us on the telephone. We won't answer. Don't send any gifts for the baby you helped us adopt. We'll send them back unopened."

His parents are godly people. His father has been a pastor for years. Their hearts were broken. But they have never stopped trying. They still send presents at Christmas. They send birthday cards. They write to tell their son what is happening in their lives. They are staying on the path of reconciliation, not burning any bridges. I don't know if that relationship will ever be restored, but I do know they are doing everything possible to restore it.

Help the other person if you have the opportunity. Look for ways to be his friend. Be kind if you meet him. Keep praying for him. When someone leaves our church, I never take him/her off my prayer list until I know for sure that I don't have a single twinge of hard feeling toward that person. When I truly want God to bless him, I know my attitude toward him is what it should be.

Following these steps will help restore the broken relationships that come to all at times. When you are faced with a ruptured relationship, the pattern to follow is David's behavior in his relationship with Saul.

Chapter 8
Recovering From Rejection

"Now Jephthah the Gileadite was a mighty man of valour, and he was the son of an harlot: and Gilead begat Jephthah.

"And Gilead's wife bare him sons; and his wife's sons grew up, and they thrust out Jephthah, and said unto him, Thou shalt not inherit in our father's house; for thou art the son of a strange woman.

"Then Jephthah fled from his brethren, and dwelt in the land of Tob: and there were gathered vain men to Jephthah, and went out with him."—Judg. 11:1–3.

Jephthah is a prime example of one who suffered from rejection. It's important to realize from the very beginning that his rejection was without basis. Whose fault was it that Jephthah was the son of a harlot? His parents. Jephthah had nothing to do with it. Innocent individuals shouldn't bear any blame for things that aren't under their control. But frequently it happens, and they experience the pain of rejection.

Jephthah's half brothers didn't want anything to do with him. They cast him out of the house so that they wouldn't have to share their inheritance. There would come a day when they turned to him for help, but the pain of rejection that he had suffered as a young man colored Jephthah's response and led him to make a very foolish vow that damaged his family.

There are several principles in the story of Jephthah that help us understand where rejection comes from and how we should respond to it properly.

I. The Presence of Rejection

Virtually everyone has felt rejected at some point in his life. Maybe another child was favored by his parents. Perhaps a teacher treated someone else in the class better. Whatever the cause or the setting, the pain of rejection is very real.

Causes of Rejection

Some people are rejected because of their background. Often they are rejected because of their race, social status, appearance, abilities or lack thereof. Nobody should ever be rejected for any of those reasons.

The things that unite us in the family of God are far greater than anything that could divide us. If a person is handsomer than someone else, that doesn't make him any better in God's eyes. The lack of physical beauty or attractive appearance shouldn't make anyone matter less to us. James 2 tells us that judging someone because of their appearance is a sign of evil thinking.

Jephthah had nothing to do with the situation that led to his rejection. It wasn't his fault that his mother was a harlot and his father had been immoral.

It's interesting that his brothers didn't criticize their father. I believe it was because they were focused on the inheritance they would get from him. They used the circumstances of Jephthah's birth against him because they didn't want Jephthah to have any part of the inheritance.

Sometimes people are rejected because of their behavior. To a certain extent we have some control over whether people reject us because of our behavior. But it isn't always because of bad behavior that we are rejected. David was rejected by Saul because of his good behavior. He did nothing to justify the way Saul treated him.

The Prodigal Son was rejected by his brother because of bad behavior. He took his father's money and wasted it in pursuing pleasure in wicked living. His brother resented that and refused to welcome him when he returned home.

When we are rejected, we need to examine our behavior and see if we have done something that might explain the rejection. If the rejection is due to our bad behavior, we need to take steps to make things right. But if our behavior does not justify rejection, we can be confident knowing that we are not to blame for the situation.

Jesus talked about this kind of situation in the Sermon on the Mount. He said, "Blessed are ye, when men shall revile you, and persecute you, and shall say all manner of evil against you falsely, for my sake" (Matt. 5:11). The rejection that comes because of good behavior brings us a blessing from God. We should never allow that kind of rejection to alter the way we act.

Conduits of Rejection

There are many ways rejection can come into our lives.

Rejection can come from our family. This was the case of Jephthah. Those who should have been closest to him turned their backs on him completely. There is probably no more painful rejection than that which comes from our own flesh and blood.

I was really close to my cousin Jimmy when I was a boy. We lived many miles apart, but we were born within a few weeks of each other. When Jimmy was about twelve, he had to write a paper for school. He worked hard writing about a day he went fishing with his father. His dad didn't usually have much time for his wife or children, so that was a special day to Jimmy. But instead of being impressed with the paper, his dad criticized it. The next time we were together, Jimmy told me about it. I'll never forget his words: "You'd think he'd want to be proud of me."

Sometimes rejection comes from our friends. Those we have depended on and relied on the most can turn away from us. The Prophet Zechariah foretold what would happen to Jesus: "And one shall say unto him, What are these wounds in thine hands? Then he shall answer, Those with which I was wounded in the house of my friends" (Zech. 13:6).

Sometimes rejection comes from our foes. Although this kind of rejection is not as painful as other kinds, it still stings. The danger in dealing with rejection from our enemies is that we are tempted to compromise our beliefs and standards in order to be accepted. This never works. Our enemies will not accept us even if we lower ourselves to their level.

II. The Products of Rejection

Let's look at a few common products, or results, of rejection.

Confusion

People who have been rejected don't know who loves them, who is for real, whom they can trust or whom to believe. They're suspicious of others' actions and motives, because they've been hurt before and don't want to be hurt again.

On the other hand, they tend to be desperately eager for some kind of acceptance. They're willing to take great risks in order to belong.

When men of Gilead came and asked Jephthah to lead them into battle, he leaped at the chance. Jephthah didn't ask whom they were fighting, what kind of army their enemies had, or what the risks involved were. The only thing he wanted to know was if they were serious about their offer to give him leadership if he won the battle.

Years ago we were involved in a court case regarding our Christian school. One of the witnesses was a psychologist. He had studied extensively the effects of being taught in an environment that didn't share the same values the students were learning at home. He stated that he had observed three likely outcomes in such a scenario.

Student's can reject the school's values and accept what they learn at home. This makes them hate the school. They can accept the school's values and reject what their parents have taught them. This makes them hate their parents. But he testified that the most likely outcome is that they try to conform in both places. They attempt to fit in with two different value systems depending on where they are.

He concluded that in such cases, the students don't hate the school or their parents. Instead, they wind up hating themselves.

Contention

People who have suffered rejection don't trust others easily. They find it easier to fuss and argue than to get along with others. They come to every relationship with their fences up. They have a chip on their shoulder. They are willing to fight at the drop of a hat—and they will drop the hat.

Many times I counsel those struggling with a quick temper or a sharp tongue. As we probe to discover the root cause of their problem, so often it turns out that they were rejected and have not dealt with that issue. It shows up in the way they deal with others. Because they have not received grace and acceptance from others, they find it very difficult to extend it to others.

Compliance

People who have been rejected often reach out for acceptance. They are so desperate for someone to give them attention that they will do almost anything to get it. These people are looking for somebody to tell them they belong. Their loneliness and pain drive them to agree to do things, even things that they know are wrong, so they can have someone who will accept them.

Over the years I've counseled a number of women who were living in immoral relationships with men. Usually these men were bums. It was not uncommon for these women to be supporting the men financially. These were not the kind of women you would expect to be immoral. Often they had grown up in church. For a long time I didn't understand why anyone would be willing to live like that. Sometimes they would end one relationship and jump right into another that was as bad or worse.

I finally learned that the thing motivating their behavior was their desire to find somebody who would accept them.

Rejection produces a desire for acceptance that leads to a vicious cycle where things get worse and worse. Every betrayal or mistreatment confirms their belief that they don't deserve any better. They continue to search, but they will never find true acceptance in such behavior.

Corruption

Those rejected are frequently bitter people. Sometimes they are bitter at the person who rejected them; sometimes they are bitter at themselves. They feel that somehow it must be their fault. Sometimes they're bitter at God. They reason that if God really loved them, He would not have let anything so painful happen to them.

Rejection produced corruption in the life of Absalom. David refused to allow him to return to the palace after he arranged the murder of Amnon for the rape of Tamar. For five years David held him at arm's length. During that period, Absalom's bitterness over that rejection planted the seeds of his revolt against his father.

If rejection is not properly dealt with, it can lead to all kinds of sin.

III. Principles for Dealing With Rejection

Birth does not determine blessing. Jephthah was rejected because of the circumstances of his birth. It's a blessing to have a godly heritage. You can look back and thank God for your childhood and the values your parents taught you. But whether your background is positive or negative does not make you more acceptable to God.

It is a real blessing to me to have had such a godly example from my parents. I missed out on a lot of negative influences that some have had to suffer through. But that makes me no better in God's eyes. It doesn't matter if your ancestors came over on the *Mayflower* and all the men and half the women have been preachers! It doesn't make you more important, more valuable or more usable to God than anybody else.

The circumstances of your birth do not determine how worthwhile you are. They may lead others to reject you, but God never will. You can rise above where you started. When you became a Christian, God made you a new creature. Where you began life has nothing to do with how your life turns out unless you allow it to dictate your behavior.

Relative Importance of Acceptance

Some things are more important than being accepted by your adversary. Some people will do almost anything to be accepted by folks who don't even love them. Lot was Abraham's nephew. He made the trip from Ur to the Promised Land along with Abraham. He fellowshiped on a daily basis with the most godly man in the world. Yet rather than desiring the acceptance of the godly, Lot "pitched his tent toward Sodom."

Eventually he moved into the city and became a political leader. He was even willing to sacrifice his own daughters' purity and virtue to be accepted by the most wicked of men, calling them "brethren." His desire to be accepted by the ungodly corrupted him.

Lowering your standards to gain acceptance of the ungodly will destroy you, and it still won't always gain you their approval. The men of Sodom only wanted Lot for what they could get out of him.

I encourage those I'm counseling to remember that sometimes it's good that some don't like you.

At a local drugstore it seemed nobody wanted to wait on me. It wasn't because I was mean or unkind; it was because they knew I was going to witness to whoever waited on me and they didn't want to hear the Gospel. I was rejected because I was trying to be a witness and a testimony. If that happens to you, thank God!

I kept going and kept witnessing until one lady got saved. She has been a member of the church for years. Had I quit witnessing to gain the acceptance of the workers at the drugstore, that lady probably would never have become a Christian. Some things are more important than being accepted, and we should never sacrifice those things.

Realizing Why Acceptance Withheld

Rejection often has little or nothing to do with you. Some who have been badly treated by their parents tend to internalize that and wonder what is wrong with them. They wonder what made their parents be hateful toward them. These will never gain a feeling of acceptance until they realize that it probably was nothing they did that caused that rejection.

I counseled a lady who never once heard her mother tell her that she loved her. The mother lived into her eighties and gave her daughter only criticism and complaints. What had that lady done that made her mother be so mean to her?

Nothing. Conceived before her parents married, her mother was angry at her for being born!

Those who spend their whole lives trying to make up for something they never did wrong are following a recipe for disaster. When Samuel was old, the nation of Israel asked him to appoint a king over them. He was distressed because he realized that was the wrong thing to do.

But I focus attention on God's answer to Samuel: "They have not rejected thee, but they have rejected me, that I should not reign over them." There was no reason for Samuel to feel rejected. He was not the one the people were turning against.

It is proper to analyze what has happened when we are rejected. If we have done something that may have contributed to the rejection, we should try to make things right. But it may well be that the rejection has nothing at all to do with us.

Recompense Later Above Acceptance Now

It is more important to obey God than to be popular. I've witnessed to people who weren't interested in hearing the Gospel. Sometimes no one would answer the doorbell if they looked out and saw me on the porch.

I went by a house once where the family was having a cook-out. They said they had no time to listen then, so I left a tract and drove on.

Months later I received a call from a nurse at the hospital. I didn't remember the people by name, but they remembered me. Now the man was dying, and they wanted me to come. I could have said, "You didn't want to listen to me when you were well; so why ask me to come and see you now?" Of course, that's not what I said. I went to be a help and a comfort and to witness to them.

I had the privilege of leading several members of that

family to Christ. I wasn't popular when I visited them at first, but there came a day when they said, "We need the truth you have."

If you know God and know the Gospel, then people need you. That is far more important than them wanting you. Focus on what is most important rather than allowing rejection by others to get you off the track.

Reaching Too Far for Acceptance

A desire for acceptance can cloud your judgment. Jephthah didn't stop to consider the danger or the consequences of getting involved in the battle. His thought was, *If we could just win this battle, all my troubles would be over. I'd finally be accepted. People would look up to me. I'd finally get some respect. I'd be somebody.*

A lot of time people who had a tough upbringing really go out of their way to prove themselves. They have to be accepted. Frequently they pay a very high price. The desire for acceptance overrides their judgment.

Many gangs have a brutal initiation process. They require a new member to endure a beating from all the other members. Why would a person put up with such treatment? Because they want to belong more than they want anything else.

People are important. We should love them, look for ways to help them and enjoy having fellowship with them, but *only God is necessary.* A rejected person may say, "But I need...." No, you only need God. He will bring everything into your life that you need to have. Accept His provision and be satisfied with it.

Reasons for Acceptance From Some

Most people who accept or reject you do so for selfish reasons. It is part of our sinful human nature to focus on ourselves. When people come to me feeling bad about rejection, I often ask them this question to help them put things in perspective: "How many have you been a help and blessing to who give you nothing back?"

Some we want to help because they make us laugh. Sometimes we help people because it makes us feel superior. Some people show so much gratitude that it makes us feel important. Frequently we accept or reject people for selfish reasons. Others are the same way with us. Rather than allowing the rejection to derail you, reflect on the fact that they probably made that decision for their own selfish reasons.

Reciprocal Acceptance Not Always Wise

Do not base your opinion of others on their opinion of you. Jephthah was hated and rejected by his half brothers. But when they showed him a little attention and offered him acceptance, he went back to them like a yo-yo. He didn't stop to think about what was right or wrong. He didn't ask God what he should do. He didn't ask, "Will this please the Lord?" He just wanted to know if they really meant to make him their leader if he won the battle for them.

Our natural tendency is to think that those who like us are nice people. If they don't like us, then they're rotten. We like the person who is nasty to others but nice to us. We don't like the person who is good to everybody else but not to us. That is a poor basis for forming an opinion about someone's character.

Some are so very complimentary. They flatter, praise and build up with their words. Over the years I've learned that their words often can't be trusted. Just because those words are said doesn't mean we should form our opinion on that.

There are some good people who don't like me. I don't want to fall into the trap of evaluating them on that basis. I should admire, respect and appreciate good people—even if they don't respect and appreciate me.

Jephthah thought his brothers were mean, vindictive,

prejudiced, narrow-minded and petty until the day they said, "Come back and lead our army." On the day they said that, their character and nature had not changed one bit. They were still mean, vindictive, prejudiced, narrow-minded and petty. The only thing that changed was Jephthah's perception of them. Now that their bad attitudes were directed toward someone else, he thought their acceptance meant something.

Don't allow yourself to be swayed by the words or opinions of others. Base your judgments and decisions on what is right and wrong, not on what people think about you.

Rethinking Beliefs for Acceptance a Mistake

Do not let the chance of acceptance change your values. If you had asked Jephthah, "Is there anything for which you would surrender your daughter?" I believe he would have said, "No." Even if the equation had been that he could have the acceptance of his brothers, he still would have refused. But that wasn't the way the choice was presented. The chance for acceptance which was offered to him caused him to say, "I'll do anything to get this."

Jephthah made a foolish vow to God: if he won the victory, he would offer up the first thing that came out of his house on his return. He was not thinking of the cost; he was exclusively focused on gaining the acceptance of those who had rejected him.

It was only after the battle was won that Jephthah learned that the price of his acceptance was his only child. Bible scholars have debated for years on whether or not she was actually put to death. I personally do not think she was—and she should not have been. One should never make or fulfill a promise that requires you to do wrong. But in either event, the cost of Jephthah's desire for acceptance was much too high.

Some people are so bent on acquiring material possessions that they spend little or no time with their families or serving

God. When they want to succeed so they will be accepted, they often sacrifice their children in the process.

Hiel rebuilt the city of Jericho even though Joshua had pronounced a curse on anyone who did so. In I Kings, chapter 16, the Bible tells us that he "laid the foundation...and set up the gates" in his sons. We do not know for sure whether he was following the ancient pagan custom of sacrificing his own children or whether God killed them. But his desire to gain fame and acceptance by his accomplishments cost him the lives of his own children. Never allow a desire for acceptance to override what is most important.

The pain of rejection is very real. Many suffer throughout their lives because of that pain. But by applying God's remedy for rejection through these principles, we can overcome that pain and live happy and successful lives.

Chapter 9
Facing False Accusations

"And the LORD said unto Satan, Hast thou considered my servant Job, that there is none like him in the earth, a perfect and an upright man, one that feareth God, and escheweth evil?

"Then Satan answered the LORD, and said, Doth Job fear God for nought?

"Hast not thou made an hedge about him, and about his house, and about all that he hath on every side? thou hast blessed the work of his hands, and his substance is increased in the land.

"But put forth thine hand now, and touch all that he hath, and he will curse thee to thy face."—Job 1:8–11.

God was proud of Job's conduct. He was a man who was doing his very best to honor and please God. It is quite a compliment to be the person God thinks of when He wants to give a good example to the Devil.

Satan came to God and falsely accused Job. Satan is "the accuser of our brethren" (Rev. 12:10). The Devil said that Job was serving God only for the material blessings he received from God. So God allowed Satan to take away all Job had. Job lost everything. His wealth, his sheep, his camels, his oxen and even his children were all taken in one day.

The Bible says that in spite of that great calamity, Job

worshiped God. Worship literally means "kiss towards"—to direct your affection toward. Job expressed love for God in his moment of greatest tragedy. That didn't convince Satan. He didn't return to God and admit he had been mistaken. False accusers are usually not satisfied by the truth. In most cases, they are not looking for truth. They are looking to cause trouble.

Have you ever been falsely accused? Can you remember how that made you feel? What did you do about it? And how did you handle it?

The first time I remember being bothered by a false accusation was in college. I had had people say things about me before, but this one got to me. My dad told me that another student had told his father, who also was a pastor, that I hated him and wanted to beat him up. I told my dad I would never say anything like that. I didn't like or dislike this student. He wasn't even on my radar screen.

Dad said I should go to him and straighten it out. My first attitude was, *Why should I? I never said anything about him.* I honestly had no idea why that student had told his father that I hated him.

After some persuading, I finally went to him and tried to straighten things out. Years later he wrote me and apologized. We are friends now, and the matter was long ago settled. But it bothered me a lot to be accused of something I didn't do.

William Carey is considered the father of modern missions. This shoe cobbler became burdened to reach the world with the Gospel. Against great opposition, he raised the financial support to go to India as a missionary. Tragically, his wife lost her mind and accused him of terrible things. He opened himself up to a complete investigation. Those who examined him concluded there was nothing to her accusations.

Innocent people do not have anything to hide.

False accusations can create a wide variety of emotions. You can feel betrayed, hurt, angry or worried when falsely accused. To understand how we should react to false accusations, we first need to understand where those accusations originate, then look at the damage false accusations can do, and then look at both receiving and responding to them.

I. Derivation of False Accusations

What motivates people to make false accusations?

Slander

Sometimes false accusations are slanderous. They are a deliberate attempt to smear someone.

During the impeachment hearings, Paul McHale, a Democratic congressman from Pennsylvania, said that President Clinton should resign. White House officials responded by attacking McHale's record, saying that he had lied about his military service.

There was no basis for the story they released. Their only purpose was to make McHale look bad because he was attacking the president (and standing up for what was right).

Such accusations are intended to hurt and damage. Proverbs 16:28 says, "a whisperer separateth chief friends." Such a person plants rumors and innuendoes that cause doubts in people's minds.

Sincerity

Sometimes false accusations are sincere. The person may genuinely be convinced that what he is saying is true.

Years ago a preacher I know went to the grocery store with his wife. Her hair wasn't properly groomed, so she had put on a scarf. Someone accused the pastor of being out with another woman. That person was sincere but wrong. The intention was not to damage the pastor by saying something that wasn't true.

This kind of accusation is easy to respond to because if a

person is sincere, he will be satisfied when he sees there is no truth to the accusation.

When you hear a story, do what is necessary to find out whether or not it's true. Never accept a rumor or an accusation without investigating the validity of it.

Satan

Sometimes false accusations are satanic. This is what Job faced. He was being falsely accused by the father of lies.

Sometimes the Devil may have reason to accuse us; but even when we have not done wrong, that doesn't stop him. God did not accept the Devil's lies about Job. The events recorded were not the results of God's checking out Job. When the test was over, God didn't know any more about Job than He had before, but Job knew much more about God and himself.

Unfortunately, many do believe false accusations. Job's friends readily accepted as truth that Job must have done something to deserve the affliction he was experiencing.

The most damaging thing about satanic accusations is the pattern we see in the story of Job. The Devil lied about Job. After confronted by evidence showing he was wrong, he told the same lie again. Proof doesn't stop satanic false accusations.

Another deadly thing about satanic accusations is the way the Devil gets Christians to join his efforts. If you spread stories you have not investigated thoroughly, you are doing the work of the Devil. "I heard…" or, "Someone told me…" is not acceptable evidence for sharing a rumor with others. It is vitally important that we not spread false accusations, given the amount of damage they can do.

II. The Damage of False Accusations

The fallout from false accusations can have substantial consequences.

Discouragement

Job's friends joined the Devil in falsely accusing him of doing wrong. Job called them "miserable comforters." At the lowest point in his life, Job had no encouragement from his friends. When they heard about the disaster that had befallen him, they came to be with him but not to help him.

Rather than investigating the situation, these friends jumped to the conclusion that Job must be guilty of something. Their false accusations against him added to the weight of despair Job already felt.

When people are discouraged, the last thing they need is to have those who should be supporting them, believing or spreading false stories about them.

Derailment

False accusations can get people off track. Instead of keeping on with what they are supposed to be doing, those falsely accused often stop moving forward. Job did not curse God, despite the catastrophe he suffered. He did get off track, however, in trying to respond to the false accusations of his friends. His goal became to convince his friends that he was right.

The problem with this approach is that people who are trying to convince you they're sincere almost always sound insincere when they do it. Job spent his energy and time justifying himself rather than glorifying God.

When you get in trouble, whether or not the accusations are true, your main job is to give *God* a good name. Our purpose is to glorify God in times of trouble just as we should be doing when things are going well. Regardless of what is said about us, we need to focus on staying on the right track.

Destruction

Some good and sincere people are destroyed by stories that aren't true. Naboth properly refused to sell his family's vineyard to King Ahab. Jezebel consoled her wicked husband, telling him she would get the vineyard for him. She sent instructions to the elders of Naboth's city, telling them to hire evil men to make false accusations against him.

The problem wasn't just with Jezebel. The elders of the city followed her instructions and saw to it that false accusations were made against Naboth. As a result, he was stoned to death.

Any time we spread false accusations, we greatly multiply their power. Like a raging wildfire roaring through dry trees, false accusations can spread rapidly, destroying everything in their path. Ahab and Jezebel didn't get away with their evil deeds, but Naboth was still dead—destroyed by false accusation.

III. Dealing With False Accusations

How should one respond when he hears an accusation?

Receiving Unsubstantiated Accusations

If not a witness to the event, you do not immediately know whether or not the accusation is true. Whether or not you respond correctly can make all the difference in someone's life. Many accusations are not true, so do not automatically assume guilt.

First, see if the accusation is significant. There are some matters that are very serious. Issues of moral purity or doctrinal accuracy matter a great deal. Sometimes, though, accusations are made about things that, even if true, really don't make enough difference to spend time worrying about them.

The Pharisees accused Jesus and the disciples of incredibly insignificant things. They were exercised over things like whether their hands were washed properly. I told my congregation that if someone says the pastor weighs 235 instead of 230, don't let me know about it. I like my scale a little bit off! Some things do not rise to a level that deserves our attention.

Second, search out the truth. Proverbs 25:2 says that "the honour of kings [leaders] is to search out a matter." The first step is to find out if there is any basis for what has been said. It's easy to shut down the one making the charge.

Some leaders make it a policy not to listen to complaints or accusations. I believe that is a wrong attitude. The right response is to investigate whether or not there is any foundation for what is being said. Over the years I've learned that many false accusations get thrown around. I've also learned that there are many *true* accusations made.

I'm glad when people tell me about any accusation that is being made, whether it is about me or someone else. I have no chance to set the record straight unless I am told about it. So I respond in such a way that people will continue to bring matters to my attention. My standard response is to say, "I'll check it out." I then make arrangements to talk to the people involved. I find out if there are any witnesses to the charges; if so, I interview them as well. It's not a matter of not trusting a person who made the accusation; it's fulfilling the responsibility that God has given us to follow a process that will reveal the truth.

Finally, substantiate the accusation before taking any action. Sometimes there is no way to be certain what happened. Often the accusation made is the word of one person against another. It is very important to understand that God has told us what to do in such a situation. If there are only two people involved and they tell different stories, do nothing. Without corroborating witnesses, no action can or should be taken. Otherwise, everyone is at risk of being wrongly damaged by unfounded accusations.

There have been times when the issue was important enough that we used a lie detector to try to verify someone's story. The principle is, make every effort to substantiate or refute the allegation. But if you can't come to a conclusion, you can still trust God to take care of the matter.

It may be that the person is innocent and nothing should be done. Or it could be that God in His mercy plans to give him a chance to repent and make things right.

I have counseled with some who are very suspicious. They always assume the worst. My practice is to tell them, "If God wants you to deal with the matter, He will make it clear to you."

Responding to Untrue Accusations

You immediately know whether something said about you is true or false. If it is true, then seek forgiveness and make restitution. But if the accusation is false, follow a biblical model of response.

You can ignore false accusations. Jesus did not answer the false accusers hired by the Pharisees to witness against Him. "Who, when he was reviled, reviled not again; when he suffered, he threatened not; but committed himself to him that judgeth righteously" (I Pet. 2:23). If you know you have done nothing for which you need to make amends, then simply choose to trust God to ensure that things come out right.

Proverbs 26:20 says, "Where no wood is, there the fire goeth out." By responding to every little thing said about you, you can make a small situation into a much larger problem. Exercise wisdom in determining whether or not a response is necessary.

Two principles that help in making that decision are (1) How serious is the accusation? and (2) Who is making it? The messenger gives weight to or takes weight from the message. If the accusation is about a relatively minor matter or if the person making the accusation is not someone whose position or person demands an answer, it is usually best to simply ignore the accusation.

You can illuminate the false accuser. You can choose to answer the accusations and questions that are raised.

Illumination works best with a sincere accuser who is simply mistaken about what has been said. This approach also calls for prayer and judgment.

Years ago when we were building a new church building, I found that some were upset because we weren't going to pave the parking lot. We had never intended to pave the lot, but they thought we were. When they found out that was not in the plan, they became upset and said some things about my leadership.

They were wrong to talk to each other instead of coming to me. Eventually word got back to me. I found who was upset and went to them. I explained where the confusion over the paving had arisen. After I had explained the full situation, that was the last I heard of it.

In Joshua, chapter 22, is the story of the two and a half tribes who chose to stay on the east side of the Jordan River. They built an altar that was identical to the altar that God told the Israelites to build. The other tribes accused them of idol worship and threatened war against them.

The east side tribes had to explain theirs was not a false altar; it was intended to be a symbol to their children. They wanted something as a witness for future generations that they too served the true God. That explanation defused the situation. Again, it is important to remember that illumination will only work with people who are interested in knowing the truth.

You can indict the false accuser. If the person is deliberately making a false accusation, look them straight in the eye and contradict their falsehood. When the Babylonian army was attacking Jerusalem and Jeremiah was accused of trying to defect to the enemy, he said, "It is false; I fall not away to the Chaldeans" (Jer. 37:14).

A story I told earlier in the book illustrates this. Years ago a man made an extremely serious false accusation about me. Another pastor called and asked if I'd heard about it. I thanked him for telling me because I appreciated knowing the rumor was going around.

I called and spoke to the accuser. He wouldn't even confirm whether or not he had said it. I offered to pay his way to come to my church and investigate. He refused to try to find out the truth. I called my lawyer to find out what recourse I had in the situation. He said, "He's dead. Under the law, you can sue him and receive triple the amount of your damages."

While I was talking to my lawyer, the accuser's lawyer was telling him the same thing. When I talked to this man the next day, he offered to do anything he could to make things right. I asked for, and very quickly received, a notarized letter from him retracting his claim. I indicted him for making a false accusation.

Finally, you may be forced to isolate the false accuser. I don't like to be placed in this position. We work too hard to get people to come to our church to kick them out lightly. I try hard to work with people and get them to do what is right, but sometimes they refuse to listen and everything fails.

We had a member who didn't believe black people had souls. The first time I heard that, I really didn't believe he was serious. (That was what he had been taught, and he was committed to it.) No matter how many Bible verses I showed him, he refused to listen. When he began spreading that around the church, I went to him with two of our deacons and asked him not to come back again.

Paul told the church at Corinth, "I have written unto you not to keep company, if any man that is called a brother be a fornicator, or covetous, or an idolater, or a railer, or a drunkard, or an extortioner; with such an one no not to eat" (I Cor. 5:11). A railer is another name for a false accuser. A person who refuses to stop spreading falsehoods may sometimes have to be cut off from fellowship with God's people.

Dealing with false accusations about either ourselves or others is one of the unpleasant realities of life. But if done properly, we can minimize the damage. That is why responding according to Bible principles is so important for each of us in these situations.

Chapter 10
God Knows What He Is Doing

Most of us would have called it sacrifice. They thought it was an exciting opportunity.

In 1921, David and Svea Flood left Sweden with their two-year-old son to serve God in the Belgian Congo. Along with another Scandinavian couple, the Ericksons, they left the main mission station in order to bring the Gospel of Christ to a remote village named N'Dolera. Their sincere, devoted efforts met with disappointing resistance. Fearful of offending his pagan gods, the chief would not allow them to enter the village. Discouraged but still committed, the two couples moved half a mile away and built their own huts. Though they prayed earnestly for God to give them an open door of opportunity to reach the needy village, nothing happened.

The only contact these sincere, dedicated young missionaries had with any villager was the young boy who was allowed to sell chickens and eggs to them a couple of times each week. Svea Flood, diminutive in stature at only four feet, eight inches tall, but large in heart, decided that since this young man was the only African to whom she had access, she would seek to lead him to Christ. She did. But there were no other converts, no other opportunities.

Malaria began to afflict the Ericksons and the Floods.

Eventually, the Ericksons decided to return to the main mission station, leaving David and Svea in their mud hut half a mile up the hill from N'Dolera to serve alone.

Svea soon discovered that she was expecting another child. The chief found enough compassion in his heart to send a midwife to help her when the time came for the birth. Svea successfully delivered a little girl whom she named Aina.

However, already weakened from her bouts with malaria and now exhausted by the delivery, Svea survived only seventeen days before she died.

That was all David Flood could take. Something died inside of him. With his own hands, he dug a grave, placing the dead body of his twenty-seven-year-old wife inside it. He took his children back to the main mission station and handed his newborn daughter to the Ericksons. His heartache and grief were turning into anger and resentment as he said, "I'm going back to Sweden. I've lost my wife, and I obviously can't take care of this baby. God has ruined my life." With those parting words, he turned his back on his daughter, his friends, his calling and his God.

Approximately eight months later, both the Ericksons came down with a mysterious disease and died within days of each other. The baby, Aina, was given to some American missionaries who called her Aggie and brought her back to the United States to live with them when she was three years old. Aggie grew up in South Dakota with her second adoptive family. The father had taken a job as a pastor. She attended a Bible college in Minnesota, where she met a young man named Dewey Hurst, whom she later married.

Dewey eventually became president of a Christian college in Seattle, where Aggie was intrigued to find a large number of Scandinavians and a significant emphasis on Scandinavian heritage.

Aggie was surprised one day to find a Swedish religious magazine in her mailbox. She did not know who sent it and was unable to read the words. However, as she flipped through the pages, one photograph stopped her cold. The picture was of a white cross adorning a simple grave. On the cross she read the words, "Svea Flood."

Aggie immediately took the magazine to a friend who spoke Swedish and could translate for her. The friend explained that the story was about missionaries who had come to N'Dolera years earlier. He told about the birth of a baby, the death of her mother and of one young African boy who had trusted Christ as his Saviour. He went on to explain that the article told how, after the missionaries had left, the boy had received permission from his chief to start a school in the village. That boy led all of the students to Christ. The chief himself had become a believer. Now, six hundred believers lived in the village of N'Dolera.

The college where Dewy Hurst served gave him and his wife a twenty-fifth wedding anniversary present of a vacation in Sweden. While they were there, Aggie found her father.

David Flood, now an old man, had married again, fathered four additional children and become an alcoholic. He had also suffered a recent stroke. Still bitter after all these years, he had reared his family with this rule: "Never mention the name of God. God took everything from me."

Aggie met her three half-brothers and her half-sister. They seemed reluctant for her to meet the father, but they eventually said, "You can talk to him. But you need to know that whenever he hears the name of God, he flies into a rage."

The day came when Aggie entered the dirty apartment, littered with liquor bottles, and spoke to the seventy-seven-year-old man lying on a disheveled bed.

"Papa?"

David Flood turned and began to weep. "Aina! I never meant to give you away."

"It's all right. God took care of me."

The tears dried up instantly. The warmth of the moment turned cold. "God forgot all of us. Our lives have been like this because of Him." David Flood rolled over in his bed, his face set like granite, facing the wall.

Undeterred, Aggie stroked his face and said, "Papa, I've got a little story to tell you, and it's a true one.

"You did not go to Africa in vain. Mama did not die in vain. The little boy you and Mama won to the Lord grew up to win that whole village to Jesus Christ. The one seed you and Mama planted just kept growing and growing. Today there are six hundred African people serving the Lord because you were faithful to the call of God on your life. Papa, Jesus loves you. He has never hated you."

The stiffness went out of the old man's body. He rolled over and looked his daughter in the eyes. By the end of the afternoon, he was reunited not only with his daughter Aggie but also with his God.

It was several years later in London, England, at a conference on evangelism that the Hursts listened to a report given from the nation of Zaire (formerly known as the Belgian Congo). The leader of a national church spoke movingly about how the Gospel of Christ had spread through his nation and of the 110,000 baptized believers he represented.

When he finished, Aggie rushed up to inquire if this man had ever heard of David and Svea Flood.

"Yes," he said, his French words being translated into English. "It was Svea Flood who led me to Christ. I was the boy who brought food to your parents before you were born. In fact, to this day your mother's grave and her memory are honored by all of us." He began to weep and said through his tears, "You must come to Africa to see us. Your mother is the most famous person in our history."

Eventually, the Hursts did just that. Cheering throngs of villagers welcomed them. Aggie had the rare privilege of meeting the man whom her father, many years ago, had employed to carry her down the mountainside back to the main mission station. For all those involved, the most moving moment of all was when Aggie went to see the white cross adorning her mother's grave. She knelt by that primitive gravesite to pray and to praise.

In the church service later that day, the pastor quoted John 14:24 and then went on to quote Psalm 126:5.

ഇരുള

What a remarkable story about life, God and our responses! In this story is the *injustice* of a village chief who would not permit the missionaries to speak to his people, of a devoted servant of Christ dying at the age of twenty-seven, of another young missionary couple being stricken with a strange disease and dying on the mission field.

In this story we see the *disillusionment* of two young couples who come with high hopes, gospel zeal and the ideals of youth, only to find the sum total of all their sacrifice and investment one young lad who trusts Christ.

There is the *discouragement* and the *depression* of David Flood, who feels abandoned, ruined and *rejected* by his God, and the *bitterness* that settles like a cancer in his heart when he allows that discouragement to fester.

In this tale we find a young girl who could well have felt rejected by the father she had never met. And if she were like most young ladies growing up, she would have had to deal with feelings of *insecurity*. Here is also a *ruptured relationship* between a father and a daughter that is only healed on his deathbed. Here we even read of a man making *false accusations*—not against another individual but against God. Yet, through it all—through the confusion, the questions, the heartache, the despair, the sadness, the grief and the seemingly unnecessary waste of human life—we see the hand of God.

God knows what He is doing. He is always good. He is always just. He is always loving. He always works all things together for good for those who love Him and are called according to His purpose.

It is true we live in an imperfect world. We are imperfect people. But in this imperfect world, we are sustained, strengthened and succored by our perfect God.

For a complete list of books available from the Sword of the Lord, write to Sword of the Lord Publishers, P. O. Box 1099, Murfreesboro, Tennessee 37133.

(800) 251-4100
(615) 893-6700
FAX (615) 848-6943
www.swordofthelord.com